Praise for The Web-Savvy Writer

"*The Web-Savvy Writer* is an indispensable guide to the very latest trends in online book promotion, a must for any author who wants to succeed in today's competitive publishing environment. This book is jammed with information on everything from online promotion basics to emerging technologies such as podcasting, blogging, and RSS, offering detailed guidance on how to promote both your book and your career as an author."
— **Dan Poynter**, author of The Self-Publishing Manual

"*The Web-Savvy Writer* is a MUST read if you want to utilize the most cost-effective and viral methods in promoting your book like blogs, pay-per-click advertising, online reviews, ezines, and more. Patrice plows new ground filling the gap in the book promotion marketplace with her highly focused book on bringing technology to the forefront in a book marketing campaign. She's truly brilliant."
— **Scott Lorenz**, Book Publicist and President of Westwind Communications

"What is impressive about Rutledge's book is its happy blend of analytic overview and practical detail about becoming web savvy. Every page has numerous easy-to-understand suggestions that will assist an author with marketing in this web-dominated era."
— **Lee Foster**, Lowell Thomas award-winning travel author

"You have to get a copy of *The Web Savvy Writer*. I haven't underlined and highlighted a book this much since college. Whether you consider yourself an Internet novice or a web master, you will learn something from this book on every single page. So if you're serious about mastering the art of online promotion, buy it right now! I didn't know how much I didn't know until I bought this book!"
— **Louise Knott Ahern**, Principal, The Working Writer Communications

"*The Web-Savvy Writer* is required reading for all authors serious about promoting themselves in today's digital age. With so many options available—websites, blogs, podcasts, ezines, and more—the mere thought of creating a high-tech game plan is a daunting task for most writers. Not anymore! Patrice takes you by the hand through the key elements of a digital promotion plan, turning confusing concepts into easy-to-understand, easy-to-apply strategies. This book is worth its weight in gold!"
— **Kay Lockner**, Founder, AuthorMBA

The
Web-Savvy Writer:
Book Promotion with
a High-Tech Twist

Second Edition

Patrice-Anne Rutledge

Pacific Ridge Press

The Web-Savvy Writer: Book Promotion with a High-Tech Twist, Second Edition

International Standard Book Number: 978-0-9778304-2-8
Library of Congress Catalog Card Number: 2008937732

Second Printing: October 2008, revised
First Printing: July 2006
Printed in the United States of America

Book cover by helGaRAPHICS.com

Table of Contents

Dedication

To my mother, Phyllis L. Rutledge, for all her love and support

About the Book

It's been said that more than 80 percent of all people want to publish a book. As a published author, or soon-to-be-published author, you're one of the rare few who have actually made this dream a reality. But publishing your book is only the first step. Promoting your book is the next, and often larger, step. Reaching out to the Internet's more than one billion users is one of the best ways to easily and inexpensively promote your book to your target audience. Creating a successful online book promotion strategy, however, can be a daunting task for many authors. What you need is a commonsense approach to online marketing, specifically focused on how you, as an author, can tap the power of the Internet to expand your publicity, platform, *and* profits.

Profit and Prosper Through Online Book Promotion

The Web-Savvy Writer: Book Promotion with a High-Tech Twist, Second Edition shows you how to develop a cost-effective, targeted online book promotion campaign, assuming no prior technical skill other than basic computer knowledge. In this book, you'll learn how to:

- Develop a website that drives book sales
- Create an attention-getting online media campaign that attracts both the press and potential readers
- Plan and conduct a successful virtual book tour that reaches thousands more potential book buyers than any in-person tour
- Profit from new media such as blogging, podcasting, and web video that enable you to develop and maintain an audience and your all-important author platform
- Save time and money by choosing the most cost-effective products and services and automating your online book promotion campaign
- Learn by example, with dozens of sample scenarios that help you quickly put technique into action
- Master the world of social networking sites like MySpace, YouTube, Facebook, and more to generate word-of-mouth buzz for your book
- And much more!

Real World Web-Savvy

The Web-Savvy Writer is filled with ideas and examples of how you can use online marketing techniques and technologies to promote your book. The Web-Savvy in Action sections offer examples of fictitious authors who use the techniques discussed in each chapter. Although the examples are intended to give you ideas for implementing these online marketing techniques in the real world, neither the authors nor their books actually exist in real life.

The Author Profiles appendix introduces you to 12 real authors who are successfully promoting their books online. Some use all the cool new technologies to promote, whereas others follow a more traditional approach to online book promotion. In either case, they have found a way to work the web for their benefit. Read their stories for motivation and inspiration for your own online book promotion efforts.

Your Online Path to Success

I've been an author and technology journalist for the past ten years and have used online marketing techniques extensively to promote my books and writing career. These efforts have resulted in the publication of 26 books, increased sales, numerous interview requests, speaking engagements, and high Google keyword ranking for my book companion websites. In a way, I owe much of my career success to the Internet. It's been my online path to success and can be yours too by following the techniques described in this book.

The Web-Savvy Writer on the Web

The Web-Savvy Writer website (**www.websavvywriter.com**) keeps you up-to-date on the ever-changing world of online book promotion. It offers:

- News on the latest trends in book promotion and publishing
- Free articles on online book promotion
- Subscription forms to my blog feed and ezine
- Information about new books, CDs, and events

About the Author

Patrice-Anne Rutledge is a bestselling author, successful technology and lifestyle journalist, and online book promotion expert who uses websites, blogs, and other online marketing techniques to promote her books and writing career. Patrice has authored 26 nonfiction books for leading publishers including Pearson, Macmillan, Prentice Hall, Random House, and Ziff-Davis Press.

In addition to *The Web-Savvy Writer*, she is the author of *The Truth About Profiting from Social Networking*, which received endorsements from leading industry experts. Her book on presentation technologies, *Special Edition Using Microsoft Office PowerPoint 2007*, received rave reviews from CEOs in the communications industry, including InFocus and IABC. Her book on desktop design, *The Essential Publisher Book*, was named one of Amazon.com's top design books of the year. Other titles include *Your Home Office* and *Smart Travel*. Many of her books have been translated and are currently available in 11 languages.

Patrice has also contributed hundreds of articles to magazines, newspapers, and websites around the world. Her work has appeared in *Smart Solutions, Dot-Com Builder, Microsoft OfficePro, Microsoft Office Solutions, Small Business, Interactive UK, Career Woman, CompuServe Magazine European Edition, InformIT,* and *ZDNet.* In addition, she founded the newsletter *Global Business Technology Report,* one of the first publications to focus on the use of online and web technologies in international business.

In her professional career, Patrice has managed a wide variety of online communication programs for leading technology firms. She is a specialist in global business communications and communication technologies including blogging, podcasting, search engine optimization, webcasting, and online public relations. She holds the designation of Certified eMarketer (CeM).

You can reach Patrice at patrice@patricerutledge.com.

Introduction

The Wave of the Future—
Online Book Promotion

The web is where you want to be if you're serious about promoting your books in the 21st century. More than one billion people worldwide use the Internet and over 200 million of them have bought a book online. Many more have learned about a book online and purchased it in a local store. Online book promotion is the best way for authors to reach this large, global audience at a low cost. From basic techniques such as creating a website to emerging technologies like podcasting, RSS, videoblogging, and web multimedia, there's a way to attract attention and publicity for your book online. A world of opportunity awaits authors who work the web and profit by doing so. You just need to get started ...

Quick Fact	In 2007, more than 400,000 new books were released in the U.S. including approximately 280,000 commercially released titles and 135,000 on-demand titles. —*Source: R.R. Bowker*

Online Book Promotion as Your Competitive Edge

Just reading the statistics on the sheer number of books published over the past few years illustrates the competition every author faces. It's hard to stand out from the crowd, particularly if you're the author of a midlist book whose publisher offers little promotion for your title. If you self-published, the entire promotional effort is up to you. This means that today's authors *must* self-promote to ensure the success of their books.

One of the major advantages of online book promotion is that its reach is worldwide. If you're lucky, a signing in a local bookstore could attract 20 people. An online campaign has the potential of reaching anyone with an Internet connection. Obviously, you can't market to the entire universe of Internet users, but a ready audience on the web is interested in your book's topic. The goal of online book promotion is to find this audience, connect with them, and encourage them to buy your books and related products and services.

The other advantage of online book promotion is that it's cost-effective. When you consider the expense of purchasing print ads or mailing thousands of brochures and media kits, the cost of promoting online is very small in comparison.

Most of the suggestions in this book aren't expensive, even if you decide to outsource some of the work to others. Some of the ideas cost nothing. There are even ways for the web-savvy author to recoup the minimal expenses of website, blog, and podcast hosting.

Standing Out from the Crowd

Finding a way to stand out from the crowd is critical to the success and profitability of any online book promotion campaign. Ten years ago, just having a website was enough to attract attention. Today, podcasts are drawing a crowd. Five years from now, some new technology will emerge. The point is that you need to be ahead of the competition to get your book noticed.

Some of the techniques I discuss in this book are a must for every author, such as creating your own website. Others are in the early adopter stage, but that's even more reason to get involved sooner rather than later. Several years from now, these ideas may become as commonplace as a website or an email newsletter. If so, you'll have had time for your campaign to take root and lead the pack instead of following your competitors, wishing you had done something back when you first thought of it.

Know Your Options

The ideas and suggestions in *The Web-Savvy Writer: Book Promotion with a High-Tech Twist, Second Edition* target traditionally published authors, self-published authors, and authors who want to promote supplemental products such as ebooks, special reports, and audio CDs.

Keep in mind, however, that what you're allowed to do depends on whether you own the rights to your content or your publisher does. For self-published books for which you own the ISBN and other information products you create independently, you have the right to promote and sell in any manner you please.

If you want to promote a book published with a traditional publisher, remember that:

- Your publisher will handle the distribution of your book, for example, making it available in bookstores, in online stores, and in additional formats such as ebook versions. Your focus should be on promotion, not distribution.
- Ask permission from your publisher before posting excerpts. If you ask, they can usually provide you with PDFs.
- Get to know your assigned publicist. Find out what this person has planned for your book and indicate your willingness to participate in promotional efforts.

Understand that, unless you're a top author or wrote a book on a particularly hot topic, your publisher probably won't be able to do extensive publicity on your title. Publishers encourage authors to get involved in the promotion of their books. They welcome your efforts as long as you don't violate the terms of your contract, have unrealistic expectations of your publicist, or become overly assertive when discussing the promotion of your book. In other words, be reasonable and treat your publisher as a partner in your writing career for optimal results.

Getting Started with Online Book Promotion

Getting started with online book promotion takes little more than basic computer skills and a desire to learn. You don't need to be a technical genius to promote your book online, but you do need to possess basic computer literacy. Fortunately, most authors already have a firm command of the basics such as how to use common software applications, send email, access the Internet, and perform web searches. From there, a willingness to develop new skills—or outsource to someone who already has these skills—will help you continue on your journey.

As you read this book, you'll probably develop a long list of ideas for promoting your own work. You'll also probably feel energized, excited, and perhaps a bit overwhelmed. At this stage, it's important to remember that online book promotion is an ongoing process, not a one-time task. Focus on the basics first. Then continue adding new promotional techniques based on your own interest level and what reaches your target audience best. Creating a plan over the course of several months, or even a year, can help prevent you from becoming overwhelmed with all of the possibilities—and help you generate more positive results.

Now, let's get started …

1

Promoting Your Book with a Website

A website is the core and starting point of any online book promotion campaign. Despite the current popularity of blogs, podcasts, and ezines, your website is still your primary online "home" for information on your book.

The following are some examples of what you can do with a focused, quality website:

- Drive book sales for traditionally published books
- Sell self-published books directly to the public
- Sell supplemental products, such as audio CDs, DVDs, courses, and special reports
- Develop a community for your readers
- Position yourself as an expert on a specific topic
- Market related consulting, speaking, and coaching services
- Display an online portfolio of writing samples if you also work with editorial or commercial clients

Quick Fact	About 72 percent of American adults use the Internet, which translates into approximately 145 million people. Of those online, 91 percent send email, 90 percent use a search engine to find information, 27 percent read blogs, 67 percent buy products online, and 72 percent get news. —*Source: Pew Internet & American Life Project*

Planning Your Website

Before you create your website, you should educate yourself about website basics and map out a blueprint for your content and design.

Understanding Website Basics

It's important to understand basic terms such as ISP, web hosting, and domain names before making any decisions about the services you need to publish your website.

An Internet Service Provider (ISP) is a company that provides Internet access, through dial-up, high-speed DSL/cable, or wireless. Popular ISPs include Comcast, Verizon, AOL, SBC, and EarthLink. A web host is a company that provides server space and related services, commonly referred to as web hosting services. Through a web host, you can register your own domain name for your site, such as **www.patricerutledge.com**, and publish your site on the web.

Many ISPs offer web hosting services in addition to Internet access, but not all do. Popular web hosts include Go Daddy, HostGator, and Yahoo! Even if your ISP offers web hosting, you can still choose a different web host that provides better pricing or services.

Tip
Some ISPs offer a free website with your Internet access account, but these rarely include all the web-hosting features a professional site requires or offer your own domain name. For example, let's say your ISP is Really Cool ISP. The URL your ISP provides for the free website could be something like **www.really-cool-isp.com/~patricerutledge**. This might be fine for personal use, but not for business use. Instead, you should register your own domain name (such as **www.patricerutledge.com**) and host your site with a web host.

Determining What Drives Your Site

When you plan the structure and content of your site, one of the first things to determine is what drives your website:

- On a **personality-driven site**, the author is the draw. This is most common for fiction writers or authors of creative nonfiction in which who you are is more important to readers than the specific subject matter you cover.
- A **platform-driven site** is most common with nonfiction authors who are experts in a particular niche and offer a book (or a series of books) on this topic in addition to related products and services such as consulting, speaking engagements, audio CDs, and special reports.
- A **book-driven site** is appropriate for authors who have written a single book or multiple books on unrelated topics. In this case, the book itself is the draw.

Determine what your driver is and then build your site around this focus.

Establishing Your Audience and Goals

Any book website has at least two audiences: your readers and the media. Be sure to design a site that meets the needs of both. For your main site content, develop a profile of your target reader, and focus your site on this profile. Are you targeting new parents, travelers to Italy, or fans of romantic suspense?

In addition, you should establish site goals. Are you primarily interested in selling books? Or do you want to sell other products and services as well? Are you hoping to garner major media coverage or establish yourself as a professional speaker? Write down your target audience and goals and keep these in mind as you plan your site.

Content Is King

Now that you've determined what drives your site and have a clear idea of your target audience and the goals you want to achieve, it's time to start thinking about your content. The right content can make the difference between a high-traffic site that drives the sale of books, products, and services and a site that receives few visitors.

The following are several tips for creating quality web content:

- Map out your page content before even starting any site design.
- Determine the goal for each page on your site and create content that supports that goal. For example, you may have pages that are informational and others there to generate sales for your books and products. Truly informational pages usually take on a more journalistic tone, but sales-oriented pages should have a call to action.
- Remember that you're writing for the web, not another medium. If you're not an experienced web copywriter, consider learning more about writing for the web. A good book to consider is *Web Copy That Sells* by Maria Veloso (AMACOM, 2004).
- The design supports the content; the content doesn't support the design.

This section provides numerous content ideas for your site, both required and optional.

Your Book: Core Content for Your Site

The core component of any author website centers on the books you've written. Regardless of what else your site promotes, your book is essentially your "calling card" and you must present it strategically on your site.

Basic Book Information

One of the key elements of an author website is to provide information about your books. How you position this depends on what drives your site and how many books you've written. Obviously, if you've written a single book then that book should be the main focus. If you've written multiple books, you'll probably want to highlight your latest book on your home page and have a link to information about each of your other books. Basic book information includes the following:

- A summary of your book's subject matter or plot
- Details such as page count, price, publisher, ISBN, and publication date
- Information on how to purchase your book

Your book's main information page is a good place to practice your copywriting skills. You need to write tight, focused copy about your book's benefits to spark reader interest and generate sales.

Tip	Many authors choose to provide a link to Amazon.com where readers can purchase their books. If you join the Amazon Associates program, in addition to your regular royalties, you can receive a 4 percent commission on every sale directed from your site.

▸ See chapter 8, "Selling and Promoting Your Book on Amazon.com"

Book Excerpts

Posting an excerpt is an excellent way to give potential readers an opportunity to learn more about your book and, hopefully, encourage them to purchase it. The most common format for online book excerpts is PDF, which stands for Portable Document Format. Using any operating system, you can view PDF documents with the free Adobe Reader software, which most computer users already have installed on their computers. If you don't have a copy, download one for free at **www.adobe.com/products/acrobat/readermain.html**.

If you published your book with a traditional publisher, ask if you can post an excerpt on your website. Many publishers will provide a PDF excerpt for you. Posting your excerpt on other websites can also create buzz for your book. Working through my publicist, I was able to post excerpts of my latest PowerPoint book on several high-traffic sites, which helped increase sales and visibility.

If you self-published your book, you should be able to get a PDF from the company that designed your book pages. Otherwise, it isn't difficult to create your own PDFs. The ability to generate PDFs is also useful if you want to create ebooks, reports, or any other type of electronic document.

For nonfiction books, consider posting the first few pages of each chapter to give readers an idea of what your book covers. For fiction, it's best to post the first chapter in order to capture readers' attention and encourage them to read your entire book.

Tip	Creating your own PDF is easy. You can use the Create Adobe PDF Online service (**createpdf.adobe.com**) and create your first five PDFs at no charge. After that, you can sign up for monthly or annual plans and create as many PDFs as you want. Alternatively, consider a third-party PDF creation tool such as Nitro PDF Professional (**www.nitropdf.com**), pdfFactory (**www.pdffactory.com**), or PDF Converter (**www.nuance.com/pdfconverter**). Another option is the free Microsoft Save as PDF or XPS add-in (**www.microsoft.com/downloads**) if you use Microsoft Word or Publisher 2007.

Book Table of Contents

A table of contents is a necessity for a nonfiction book. Readers, reviewers, and journalists looking for experts want to know more about your book. You can post your table of contents as text on your site or as a PDF.

Book Reviews

If your book has been reviewed, mention it. You can link to online reviews, list or post print reviews, or extract any particularly glowing comments to display prominently on your site.

Book Endorsements and Testimonials

Have you amassed a collection of stellar testimonials about your book? Has a well-known expert or celebrity given you a positive endorsement? Include these words of praise on your website. However, be sure to ask first so that people aren't surprised when they see their name online.

Video Book Trailer

Creating a book trailer to bring your book to life is an investment in both time and money, but there is a solid payoff for many authors. Trailers combine audio, video, text, and still images and can hold visitor attention better than static text alone.

▸ See chapter 10, "Promoting Your Book with Audio and Video," Video Book Trailers

Reading Group Guides

Reading groups, both online and offline, are increasingly popular. If your book is a good choice for a reading group, offer a reading group guide on your site.

Additional Content Ideas for Your Site

In addition to focusing on your books, you should consider the following content ideas to round out your site.

Your Biography

A bio is a critical part of any author website, and every site should have one. Whether you're trying to reach readers, the media, or potential clients, people want to know who you are. There are essentially two types of bios:

- **Traditional bio.** A traditional bio is useful for authors who want to emphasize their credentials. Most nonfiction authors fall into this category.
- **Narrative bio.** The narrative approach works particularly well for authors of fiction or creative nonfiction who essentially want to tell a story through their bio.

When writing your bio, consider your audience. If your goal is to sell books on financial planning (as well as fill your seminar seats and get hired for speaking engagements), your bio needs to reflect your expert qualifications as a financial planner. If you're trying to encourage potential readers to buy your mystery novel, create a bio that piques the interest of a mystery fan.

Also, consider creating both a long bio (multiple paragraphs) and a short bio (a few sentences) to use for different purposes.

Web-Savvy In Action

Braden is the first-time author of a literary novel set in an Alaskan fishing village that explores the universal themes of trust and betrayal. He doesn't have a following yet, so his book is the main focus of his website. With permission from his publisher, Braden posts the first chapter of his novel as a PDF excerpt to interest potential readers. He also includes an Amazon Associates link to purchase his book online.

His novel has received many positive reviews as well as an endorsement from a well-known novelist, which he prominently highlights on his website. Because Braden is a native Alaskan, he creates a narrative bio that relates to his own unique childhood as well as the setting and themes of his book. Finally, Braden creates a reading group guide to tap into the reading group market he feels would have an interest in his book.

Résumé and Credentials

Many authors include a résumé or a list of credentials on their websites. This is particularly important for nonfiction authors whose credibility relies on solid professional expertise or authors who offer consulting or related services.

If your work history is important to potential clients or readers, create a traditional résumé that includes a list of your writing credits. Another option is to create a backgrounder. It's similar to a résumé, but emphasizes qualifications and writing credits over jobs held. A backgrounder could include the following:

- Name and contact information
- Areas of specialties
- List of book credits
- List of article credits
- Summary of work experience
- Other relevant skills
- Professional credentials

You can include a résumé or backgrounder in text format on your site, as a Word document, or as a PDF. Text and PDF are the most common formats, and some authors include both.

▸ See "Book Excerpts" in this chapter

Tip

Remember, anyone on the Internet can read what you post in an online résumé or backgrounder. Pay attention to the level of personal information that you include. In general, it's best to avoid listing your physical location unless it's a business address. Renting an inexpensive mailbox is one way to provide address information without disclosing the location of your personal residence.

Frequently Asked Questions (FAQs)

Posting a list of questions and answers provides more personalized, detailed information than a bio can offer. When constructing your FAQ, include questions that offer background information not found in your bio, position yourself as an expert in your field, and relate directly to what you want to promote (for example, your book, consulting services, and so forth) without overtly sounding like an advertisement. Alternatively, post answers to the most common reader questions that you receive.

Online Portfolio

If you contribute to magazines and newspapers in addition to writing books, you'll probably want to create an online portfolio. An online portfolio serves as a web-based showcase for your writing samples also referred to as clips. Displaying writing samples online is a key goal for many writers. There are several ways to handle the issue of clips on a website:

- Display clips as text on a web page
- Display clips as PDFs

- Link to external clips on other websites
- Create a combination approach

▶ See "Book Excerpts" in this chapter

Blog and Podcast Links

If you publish a blog or podcast, include links from your main website.

▶ See chapter 3, "Promoting Your Book with a Blog"
▶ See chapter 5, "Promoting Your Book with a Podcast"

Recorded Audio Messages

If you think you can reach your target audience through the spoken word, consider posting a recorded audio message. For example, you may want to post a website greeting, introduce the topic of a book you published, or read a passage from a work of fiction or poetry.

▶ See chapter 10, "Promoting Your Book with Audio and Video," Promoting with Audio

Ezine Subscription Form

If you have an ezine (online newsletter), include a subscription form on every page of your website. An ezine is one of the best ways to collect the names and email addresses of your readers and keep in contact with them on an ongoing basis.

▶ See chapter 6, "Promoting Your Book with an Ezine"

Latest News

Readers and the media like to know about your latest books, appearances, and other projects. Having a "What's New" section or page keeps your audience informed and promotes your latest work.

Interactive Content

Interactive games, quizzes, and brief web videos can enliven your site and help you interact with site visitors. Be sure to balance the excitement of multimedia, however, with the impact it has on how quickly your site loads. Fortunately, several options exist for adding intriguing content that loads quickly. Also, mix in text-based interactive content, which can add excitement without any impact to site performance.

▶ See chapter 10, "Promoting Your Book with Audio and Video"

List of Services

If you offer consulting, coaching, speaking, or other writing services related to your area of expertise, be sure to highlight these services on your site.

List of Credits and Clients

Listing writing credits and clients is another common component on an author's website. It can also help define your expertise in a particular specialty.

Contact Information

Even with great credentials, you can lose sales and assignments if your site visitors don't know how to reach you. Make it easy for readers, journalists, editors, agents, and potential clients to get in touch with you. In general, prominently displaying your email address is probably sufficient contact information.

If you have a business, you may want to add your phone number and business address as well. Contact information can be at the bottom of every page of your site or on a special contact page. A form is another way to let your site visitors contact you.

Resource Center

As a service to site visitors, many authors include a list of related links. This can be as simple as a single page with categorized groupings of links. Alternatively, devote a multi-page section to links and resources. Some authors even create a separate website related to their topic of interest. Including affiliate links in your resource list is a source of additional revenue for many authors.

▶ See chapter 10, "Promoting Your Book with Online Advertising," Affiliate Marketing Revenue

Web-Savvy In Action

Angel is an author who specializes in spa travel. She creates two websites. One is an author site focusing on her travel guidebooks. The other is an informational site dedicated to spa travel with solid information of real value to her target audience. On the spa travel site, Angel includes tips and short travel articles, links to her books, and a collection of resources related to spas and spa travel. Through the careful use of affiliate links and paid advertising for travel products she recommends, not only does Angel provide a service to her readers, she generates added revenue as well.

Calendar of Events

If you do many personal appearances to promote your writing, speak at conferences, participate in radio or TV interviews, or conduct training seminars, posting a calendar of your activities is a must. You can get creative and design an actual calendar with search capabilities, but a simple list suffices for all but the most active speakers. Listing your prior appearances also helps promote your professional reputation.

Related Products and Services

Selling related products and services through your website offers the opportunity for multiple streams of income beyond your actual book profits. In fact, many authors actually make more money from other revenue streams than they do from their books. Nonfiction authors with a solid platform have the most options here, but a creative novelist should also be able to find ways to profit from this concept.

▶ See chapter 15, "Twelve More Ways to Promote Your Book Online," Supplemental Information Products

Freebies

In addition to free book excerpts, also consider posting other free content such as:

- Short stories (for fiction writers)
- Articles about your area of expertise
- Free tools (for example, online calculators, downloadable calendars, or workbooks)

Message Board

If you specialize in a particular topic, consider creating a message board (also known as a discussion board, group, or forum) for your audience to communicate with each other. In general, most website message boards get little traffic unless the author or topic is very popular, so consider carefully before investing time in developing a board.

Getting Graphic

Graphic images can enliven any site, but they can also be a case of too much of a good thing. Graphics slow down your site if they're too large and can actually drive away visitors with a slow connection who don't want to wait to view a graphics-intensive page.

Web graphics are usually in either a JPEG or GIF format, compressed for fast downloading over the web. JPEG, which stands for Joint Photographic Experts Group, enables you to save images with millions of colors. It is a good choice for photos. Images with flat color fields, such as most logos and book covers, compress well as a GIF, which stands for Graphics Interchange Format.

Graphics Software Solutions

If your website has more than a few graphics, you'll want graphics software to manage and edit these images. Some good choices include:

- **Adobe Photoshop (www.adobe.com/products/photoshop)**. Professional image editing software that's ideal if you have advanced skills and want a sophisticated program with a multitude of features. Photoshop, bundled with Adobe Creative Suite, is pricey, so be sure to check out the free trial before you buy.
- **Adobe Photoshop Elements (www.adobe.com/products/photoshopelwin)**. Low-cost alternative to Photoshop that enables you to edit, organize, and display photos on the web. A free trial is available.
- **GIMP (www.gimp.org)**. GIMP, or GNU Image Manipulation Program, is a free open source graphics program that offers many graphic and enhancement features.
- **Picasa (picasa.google.com)**. Free graphics software download from Google, which enables you to organize all of the graphics and photos on your computer, make basic edits, incorporate images into your blog, create slideshows, and more.

Optimizing Your Web Graphics

Web graphics need to be small. If they take too long to download, you risk losing potential site visitors—particularly those with a slower, dial-up connection. Not everyone has wireless access or high-speed DSL or cable. There are varied opinions on how quickly your website must load in order to avoid the risk of losing visitors, but, in general, it's best to try to keep your page size to no more than 30 kilobytes—including HTML and all graphics—for fast loading. In order to test how fast your page loads, try out Web Page Analyzer (**www.webpageanalyzer.com**).

If your current pages are larger than 30 kilobytes, you should optimize your graphics to make them smaller. Alternatively, consider some design changes. The following are two optimization tools to check out:

- **GIFBot (www.netmechanic.com/gifbot/optimize-graphic.htm)**. A free graphics optimization service sponsored by NetMechanic that allows you to optimize only one graphic at a time.
- **SiteScan (www.optiview.com)**. A web-based tool that scans your website for large graphics, duplicate graphics, and broken links. It then returns smaller, optimized graphics, which you can use to replace your large files. Monthly subscription pricing is on a sliding scale based on the size of your site and the frequency of scanning.

Tip	Another way to ensure faster page loading is to reuse images. For example, let's say that you display an image of your book cover on numerous pages in your website. Instead of placing this graphic in multiple directories or creating copies of the same graphic under different file names, you should consistently link to the same graphic image.

Graphics for the Media

Small graphics that work well on the web usually don't work well for print. If you want to post graphics for the media to use, you need a different methodology. In general, the media requires high-resolution images of at least 300 dots per inch (dpi). This means the graphics you display on your site itself, such as an author photo or book cover image, need to be available at a different resolution and file size for print use.

In order not to slow down the pages that house your high-resolution images, include links to these images instead of making them viewable directly on the page. This way, only those truly interested in downloading your high-resolution images can do so.

Your Photo

An author photo enhances your website and helps you reach out to your audience. People like to know more about authors, and your photo can help readers connect to you. Choose a photo that reflects the image you want to portray through your writing.

For authors who cover business or professional topics, a standard headshot usually works well. If you write about sports, travel, or fitness, you could consider an action shot. Fiction authors may prefer either a standard photo or one that relates to the subject matter of their book. An animal expert could choose to be photographed with his pet.

In some cases, authors decide that posting a photo on their website just isn't right for them. For example:

- You simply don't feel comfortable posting your photo online.
- You write under a pseudonym and don't want to reveal your identity.
- Your image doesn't match the type of writing you do. You could be a woman who writes books for teen boys under a masculine pseudonym or a 90-year-old great-grandmother who writes steamy romance novels.

Unless you have true privacy concerns, however, I do recommend posting an author photo.

Images of Book and Magazine Covers

Small graphic images of your book covers or covers of magazine issues to which you've contributed give site visitors a clearer idea of your accomplishments. Your publisher or editor can usually provide you with cover images to use on your site.

Photo Gallery

Another option is to include a photo gallery. This is often popular with writers who are also photographers, such as travel writers. Other ideas include showing photos from your personal appearances such as book signings or conference presentations.

Be careful with photo galleries. If not done properly, they can look unprofessional, such as posting too many photos of your family vacations or pets, or boastful, such as pictures of you with every well-known person you've ever met. In addition, many unnecessary graphic images take up space and make your pages slow to load.

Getting the Attention of the Media with an Online Media Kit

Creating an online media kit is essential for any author looking to get the attention of the media. The content on your site may be appropriate for both your readers and the media, so you'll have to decide how to organize for maximum value. One way to handle this is to target your site to readers and then create a special section for the media to which you link from your home page. This online media kit can contain special content just for the media as well as links to content that's appropriate for multiple audiences.

The following are six ideas for content targeted specifically for the media.

Press Releases

If you've issued press releases for your book, include them in your online media kit. If you haven't created any press releases, why not? In addition to the obvious new book announcements, consider writing feature style releases that focus on your topic instead of your book itself. For example, instead of just announcing that you've written a new book on sports nutrition, create a release that provides nutrition tips for weekend athletes.

▶ See chapter 11, "Promoting Your Book with Online Press Releases"

Media Clips

If you've been interviewed in magazines, newspapers, or online publications, include details in your online media kit. Showing that you've been interviewed previously seals your expert image in the eyes of potential readers and clients and lets the media know that you're an experienced interviewee. If you've been interviewed on radio or television, consider including audio or video clips in your online media kit as well. Even if you haven't been interviewed, you can still create your own audio or video to highlight your potential as a speaker, radio guest, or television guest.

▶ See chapter 10, "Promoting Your Book with Audio and Video"

Journalist Resources

Providing journalists ready access to resources and statistics about your specialty can help make you a "go to" person in your industry.

Web-Savvy In Action

Harvey is an expert on green building who has written several books on this topic. On his website, he offers an online media kit with detailed information about his books, links to reviews and feature articles, and several recent audio and video clips.

Harvey also includes a page with detailed facts and statistics on green building as well as links to related professional associations and other web resources. In addition to providing a valuable service to consumers looking for resources, journalists covering this topic find his content of value and quote Harvey in stories on green building.

Suggested Story Ideas

Many journalists already have a firm assignment, but others welcome story ideas. In your media kit, include suggested story ideas and topics you cover.

Suggested Interview Questions

Providing a list of suggested interview questions can help you capture the media's attention as well as open the door to interviews on specific topics you'd like to discuss.

Media Contacts

You want to make it easy for the media to find you, so be sure to include detailed contact information. This can be your own contact information or that of a publicist. If you have more than one contact, use a media contacts page to clarify this. For example, you could want journalists to contact your publisher's publicity department for book review copies, but prefer they contact you directly for interviews.

Tip

If you'd rather not create your own media kit, consider a hosted online media room by BookFlash (**www.bookflash.com**). Also, look into a free listing in *BookFlash* Bulletin, an online newsletter distributed to 4,000 reviewers, editors, writers, and book professionals.

Four Ways to Design Your Site

There are essentially four options for creating your author website:

- Create your own site with a site builder
- Create your own site with blogging software
- Create your own site from a template
- Hire a website designer to design your site

No one solution is best for everyone. The option that's best for you depends on several factors, primarily your budget, level of technical skill, and timing.

Creating Your Website with a Site Builder

A site builder is a tool that many web hosting companies provide to enable the quick and easy creation of a website without the need to purchase web design software such as Dreamweaver. Most site builders let you choose a template, insert your content, and publish directly to the web. If you can format using Microsoft Word, you can use a site builder.

Although the ease of use is a draw for many people, there are some caveats. This option is quick and inexpensive, but it does have limitations. Some hosted sites have limits on the design you choose, the number of pages in your site, and, sometimes, your ability to customize your site. Questions to ask include:

- Do you have enough choice in how your site looks? Are the templates professional?
- Is there a limit to the number of pages you can include in your site? You should plan on a minimum of 10 pages for a solid website. The flexibility to expand to at least 25 pages is ideal.
- Do you get your own domain name? Or is the site an extension of the company hosting it? For example, can you use **www.patricerutledge.com** or must you use **www.really-cool-website.com/~patricerutledge**?
- Can you edit the HTML on your site? This is important if you want to edit meta tags or place ads on your site, such as Google AdSense.
- Can you incorporate ecommerce functionality?
- Is hosting included? Or is there a separate fee?

Some site builders to check out include:

- Aplus.Net WebsiteCreator (**www.aplus.net**)
- GoDaddy WebSite Tonight (**www.godaddy.com**)
- HostGator Site Builder (**www.hostgator.com**)

- Yahoo! SiteBuilder (**smallbusiness.yahoo.com/webhosting**)

Creating Your Website with Blogging Software

This is a good option for authors who want to quickly develop both a website and a blog. Most blogging tools, such as WordPress or TypePad, enable you to create pages in addition to blog posts. The flexibility of combining static pages with blog posts makes an easy-to-use blogging tool a good choice for designing your entire web presence.

Another plus is that the many blog themes and templates available eliminate the need for strong graphic or web design skills. This option is best suited to authors who have basic website needs, want to focus on blogging, and like the simplicity that blogging tools provide.

| **Tip** | The current version of Blogger doesn't enable you to add pages to your blog, so it's not the best choice if you're looking to combine your website and blog into one. |

▸ See chapter 3, "Promoting Your Book with a Blog"

Creating Your Website with a Template

This is a good alternative for do-it-yourselfers who want the experience of creating their own custom site. Templates enable you to create a quality site that follows established design standards in less time. In addition, doing the work yourself gives you control over the overall site and can save you money as compared to hiring a web designer.

Some template providers to check out include DesignGalaxy (**www.designgalaxy.net**) and Template Monster (**www.templatemonster.com**).

| **Tip** | Remember, you need to purchase the web design software specified by the template provider to customize any template. Most template providers include detailed instructions on how to customize their templates, but you still need to own and have a basic understanding of the required tools such as Dreamweaver, Fireworks, or Photoshop. |

If you plan to work from a template, determine which site design tools are required. Factor their purchase and training time into your budget. The most common include:

- **Adobe Dreamweaver** (**www.adobe.com/products/dreamweaver**). Dreamweaver is a favorite among professional web designers and is included in Adobe Creative Suite.
- **Microsoft Expression Web** (**www.microsoft.com/expression**). With the discontinuation of Microsoft FrontPage in 2006, Expression Web is Microsoft's new web design offering.

- **nVu (www.nvu.com/index.php)**. Free, open source web design software with lots of solid features.

Other popular software that web designers use include:

- **Adobe Photoshop (www.adobe.com/products/photoshop)**. Professional image editing program.
- **Adobe Fireworks (www.adobe.com/products/fireworks)**. Creates state-of-the-art web graphics. It integrates closely with Dreamweaver, but you can also use Fireworks with other applications.
- **Adobe Flash (www.adobe.com/products/flash)**. Creates interactive content.

Tip

Before investing any money into templates and software, be sure that this option is right for you. To try it out, download a sample template from your preferred template provider (most offer samples). Then download a trial version of any needed software. Major software manufacturers such as Adobe and Microsoft often offer trial versions available on their websites.

Most also provide a variety of documentation and training materials as well. This way, you can see if designing your site with professional web design tools is a good match for you without spending hundreds of dollars up front.

Hiring a Web Designer to Design a Custom Site

If you truly lack any technical or design capabilities, don't have the time to learn the skills required to do the work yourself, and want a custom site, consider hiring a qualified designer. This is the most expensive option, but it can give you a unique site that meets your exact specifications.

If you're considering hiring a web designer, one important question to ask is how to handle site updates. A static site that you rarely update can't effectively market your books. You need to be able to add new content on a regular basis, modify meta tags and text to better optimize your search engine results, and much more.

Ideally, you should "own" the content of your website and have the ability to update it as needed. If your designer used commercial software such as Dreamweaver to design your site, you'll need to purchase that software to make your own updates. Some designers prefer to retain all of your website files and have you pay them to make any required updates. Although a designer's desire to maintain control of site quality is understandable, this arrangement can become prohibitively expensive and result in a site that isn't updated as frequently as it should be.

Here are two options for avoiding the problem of expensive site updates:

- Use a service like Edit.com (**www.edit.com**) to update your website as needed.
- Request that your designer create your site using free, open source software such as nVu or WordPress. WordPress, in particular, is very easy to update once your basic site structure is in place.

Web-Savvy in Action

Polly is the author of several children's books who wants to create a fun, colorful site that matches the content of her books. She has a limited budget to spend on her website, and she doesn't have the design skills required to develop the type of site she wants. Polly decides to use a site builder and selects a template that matches the colorful, vibrant nature of her books. Using the step-by-step instructions provided, Polly quickly creates and publishes her basic site. Next, she'll learn some basic HTML so she can edit meta tags and incorporate Amazon Associates functionality.

Six Do's for Your Website

Here are six things to do when creating your website.

Use Your Own Domain Name

As a professional author, you need your own domain name. A domain name is the name used in a URL to identify your web site. For example, the domain name of my main site is **www.patricerutledge.com**. Domains usually have the following structure: www (which stands for World Wide Web), a dot, the unique domain name, a dot, and the domain suffix (such as com for a commercial site). By registering your own domain name, you avoid less professional URLs such as **www.really-cool-isp.com/~patricerutledge** as your address.

Check Out the Competition

Before you create your site, you should spend some time viewing and evaluating other author websites. This valuable competitor intelligence greatly enhances your ability to create a site that achieves your goals.

To get started, do a search on your favorite search engine for appropriate keywords, such as author website, novelist, book website, or whatever term you feel someone would use to find a site like yours. Many writers' associations also provide a list of member websites. In addition to seeking out your direct competitors, also look at the sites of authors in other genres as well as sites related to your subject matter.

▶ See chapter 15, "Twelve More Ways to Promote Your Book Online," Writers' Association Websites

Write Your Content with Search Engines in Mind

If you hope to attract traffic through search engines, keep their requirements in mind as you create your content. This is a critical step that can make the difference between a successful site and one that few people visit.

▸ See chapter 2, "Promoting Your Book with SEO"

Research Web Hosts Carefully

Choosing the right web host can be a complicated, and critical, decision. Be sure to give yourself enough time to evaluate your needs and options so you make the right choice. You can always change web hosts or plans later, but most people want to avoid the hassle of doing this often.

Some web hosts that offer many of the services author websites require include:

- Aplus.net (**www.aplus.net**)
- GoDaddy (**www.godaddy.com**)
- HostGator (**www.hostgator.com**)
- Yahoo! Web Hosting (**smallbusiness.yahoo.com/webhosting**)

The following are some tips to help you make the right choice:

- Make a list of everything you want from a web host and compare options—including features, limits, and prices—with at least three different web hosts. Creating a table can help you visually compare options.
- Carefully compare "package deals." Buying a hosting package may appear to simplify the decisions you need to make and, at times, can save you both time and money. Some packages, however, are expensive and may not deliver exactly what you need. For example, if all you need for ecommerce is an Amazon Associates account or a few simple PayPal buttons, you're better off handling ecommerce separately than choosing an expensive package with extensive ecommerce features you won't use.
- Verify everything is included in the base price and not charged per feature.
- Consider your current needs as well as future needs. Some things you can add on later without a problem, but locking yourself into a choice with little flexibility, such as a maximum number of pages, isn't a good idea.

Consider Multiple Websites

For many authors, a single website is enough to cover all aspects of your career. By carefully structuring your site, you can incorporate information on multiple books as well as on other products and services you offer.

There are times, however, when you might want to create more than one site. For example, consider multiple websites if you:

- Cover more than one distinct topic or write in more than one genre
- Want to develop a resource site for your audience
- Need to differentiate between your business and your writing career

If you plan to create multiple websites each with its own domain name, you should consider multiple domain hosting. With this type of plan, you pay one fee to host multiple domains in a single account. Companies that offer multiple domain hosting include HostGator (**www.hostgator.com**) and GoDaddy (**www.godaddy.com**).

Web-Savvy in Action	Biff is an author who specializes in South America. He has written several guidebooks as well as one novel set in the region and is considered an expert in that geographic area. Biff decides to create three websites. One is an author site focusing on his guidebooks. The second is a book website for his novel. The third is a site for travelers to South America. His travel site contains extensive travel content and provides the option to purchase books, travel gear, and tour packages. Although Biff's sites all link to each other, each is self-contained and can stand on its own.

Get Ready for Prime Time Before You Publish

There's nothing worse than a website that looks like it still needs work. Broken links and HTML glitches can send site visitors to your competitors. Before announcing a new site, be sure to verify that:

- All your links work, both internal and external
- Your graphics load properly and quickly (resize them if they load too slowly)
- There are no typos or grammatical errors in your text

If your site isn't too large, testing it manually shouldn't be too time consuming. If you have a large site, however, you may want to consider an automated tool such as NetMechanic (**www.netmechanic.com**).

Six Don'ts for Your Website

In no particular order, here are six web design sins that make me cringe:

Don't Use Frames

Frames are old web technology and you should avoid them. Few current sites still use frames and many search engines have difficulty with them.

Don't Even Consider Under Construction Signs

If your site isn't complete, don't publish it yet. Avoid site pages that contain only an "under construction" announcement. Instead, mention upcoming features on an existing page. All websites continually evolve and are under construction. Make your site visitors feel that you have it all together and are ready for business.

Don't Go Overboard on Banner Ads

Websites with numerous flashing banner ads drive away visitors. In addition, banners aren't the revenue generators they once were. Many people have become conditioned to ignore them rather than click them. Instead of loading up your site with numerous banners with the hope of generating some income, consider options such as Google AdSense and carefully chosen affiliate programs.

▶ See chapter 9, "Promoting Your Book with Online Advertising," Generating Advertising Revenue

Don't Forget Titles

One easy thing to overlook when you're creating your website is adding titles to your pages. Your web design software should explain how to create titles. If you have a problem, you can always edit the HTML directly with a title tag: `<title>My Web Page Title</title>`. Your title is the first thing that people see on a list of search results. You want the title of your page to appear, not "No Title." Creating strong page titles is also an important aspect of search engine optimization.

▶ See chapter 2, "Promoting Your Book with SEO"

Don't Get Outdated

It's 2009, and you visit a website that proudly announces a new book with the headline: "Coming Soon in April 2006!" How eager would you be to buy that book? Check your site to ensure that nothing is outdated or looks like it hasn't been revised in months.

Don't Forget to Test on Multiple Browsers

Your website may look perfect on your computer, but it may not appear the same with different browsers. If you don't test on multiple browsers, you could end up with some visitors viewing a rather ugly version of the site you worked so hard to create. Although you could test your site manually with a variety of browsers such as Internet Explorer, Netscape, Firefox, Safari, and others, it's easier to use an automated tool to do this.

Two good choices include BrowserCam (**www.browsercam.com**) and Browsershots (**www.browsershots.org**), which enable you to take automated screen captures of your site as it would appear using a variety of browsers, operating systems, and resolutions.

Website Design Step-by-Step

Creating a website that's the centerpiece of your online book promotion campaign is the first step toward success on the web. Here's your step-by-step "to do" list:

- ☐ Research website design and verify that you understand the basic concepts
- ☐ Visit competitive sites to see what works and what doesn't
- ☐ Determine your site driver, goals, and audience
- ☐ Decide what content your site will include (add phases if your original content plan looks too ambitious)
- ☐ Map out your site structure
- ☐ Decide how you're going to create your site (using a site builder, using a template, hiring a web designer, and so forth)
- ☐ Get a free trial of any software you might use and try it out before you buy it
- ☐ Research and sign up with a web host
- ☐ Select and register your domain name
- ☐ Create your site (design and structure first, then content)
- ☐ Read chapter 2 "Promoting Your Book with SEO" to learn how to optimize your site for search engines
- ☐ Test your site for broken links, errors, and browser issues
- ☐ Publish your site

2

Promoting Your Book with SEO

Search engine optimization (SEO) refers to the techniques used to achieve a top ranking in search engine results for specific keywords. Keywords are words that potential site visitors search on to find information on the web. If your site doesn't appear within the top 20 search results for a specific keyword or keyword phrase, then it's unlikely that searchers will find your site. Although SEO is both art and science, several simple things can help boost your ranking.

Quick Fact	Americans conducted 11.7 billion searches online during August 2008. Nearly 63 percent of all searches were on Google, with Yahoo! at 20.5 percent and Microsoft at 8.9 percent. —*Source: comScore qSearch*

This chapter focuses on non-paid search listings, also referred to as organic search. In addition, you can purchase search engine advertising, such as pay-per-click (PPC) ads.

▸ See chapter 9, "Promoting Your Book with Online Advertising"

Creating Your SEO Master Plan

If you have a website or blog, you should optimize it for search engines. Optimizing refers to structuring your site's content, titles, headings, and meta tags to encourage a high ranking based on the criteria that search engines use to determine site relevancy. Optimizing your site won't cost you a thing and can bring huge benefits in terms of increased traffic, so there's no reason not to add SEO to your online promotion efforts. Of course, you first need to have a plan in order to reap the rewards of targeted search engine optimization.

Search Engine Basics

Most people with access to the web are already very familiar with search engines. However, to successfully optimize your site, you need to develop more detailed knowledge than a typical user would have.

As you're probably aware, a search engine is a website on which you enter keywords related to information you want to find on the web. The search engine then displays a list of relevant websites that match the keywords you entered. A program called a spider automatically follows links on the web to compile these search results. A spider is also referred to as a crawler, robot, or bot. A search engine analyzes web pages based on a number of criteria such as titles, headings, meta tags, and actual page content. This data is then stored in an index, which is searched whenever someone enters a search request. The pages that best match the request appear at the top of the search results.

A search engine is different from a search directory, even though many people use the term search engine to refer generically to both. Real people usually compile the entries of a search directory, evaluating submissions for inclusion in specific directory categories.

Major Search Engines

Many search engines have consolidated recently, leaving a few main players with the largest market share. This is good news for authors who don't want to spend extensive time and money on search engine submission. Currently, there are three main players in the search engine world:

- **Google** (**www.google.com**). Google is the best-known search engine in use today.
- **Live Search** (**www.live.com**). Microsoft's answer to web search.
- **Yahoo! Search** (**www.yahoo.com** or **search.yahoo.com**). Yahoo! offers both a search engine and a search directory.

Depending on your geographic location and site subject matter, there are other search engines and directories to which you may want to submit your site, but the majority of your traffic will most likely come from these three sources. If you're interested in learning more about how these search engines work, check out their sites for more details.

Keyword Selection

Choosing the right keywords for your website is your first step to SEO success. Remember that unless you are particularly well known, people will search for either what you do or what you write about, not for your name, company name, or even book title.

To start, think of the target audience you want to attract to your site. What keywords would they use on a search engine to find information on your book's topic? Your website may have multiple keywords, each specific to different pages on your site.

For example, if you're a travel writer who has written guides on Ireland, Spain, and Italy, your keywords could vary depending on which country each website page covers. Your entire site can focus on one set of keywords or you can individualize keywords by page.

Web-Savvy in Action	Gabrielle is the author of a book about edible flowers. Because Gabrielle isn't well known and her book hasn't received major media coverage, it's doubtful that many people will enter her name or her book's name in an online search. Therefore, the most important keyword phrase for Gabrielle to target is "edible flowers."

Keyword Research

Once you have a list of potential keywords, it's time to do a little research to see how often people actually search on your chosen terms. Google AdWords (**adwords.google.com**) offers a free tool for analyzing potential keywords. Another service to consider is Wordtracker (**www.wordtracker.com**), a subscription-based keyword research tool that offers a free trial.

By reviewing the results and suggestions these tools provide, you can further target the most appropriate keywords for your site.

Web-Savvy in Action	Annie is the author of a wheat-free cookbook. She thinks that "wheat-free recipes" would be a good keyword phrase to target, but she wants to verify that it's a term people search for frequently. Using a keyword selector tool, she discovers that nearly 10,000 people searched on "wheat-free recipes" in the last month, which confirms her choice of this keyword phrase.

Competitor Intelligence

One final test confirms the validity of your keyword choices. Enter your keywords in popular search engines such as Google, Yahoo!, and Live Search. Then view the search results. Does the list display your competitors or unrelated websites? Not displaying your competitors can be good or bad. It could mean that your competitors have a low search engine ranking for important keywords. It could also mean that the audience you want to attract isn't using the keywords you chose.

Optimizing Your Site

With a clear understanding of the basic principles of search engine optimization and a list of keywords and keyword phrases appropriate for your site, it's time to turn your attention to actual site optimization. Exactly which techniques garner the best results is ever-changing and subject to debate, but following some basic guidelines should get you on your way to search engine success.

Optimizing Your Content with Keywords

The keywords you selected for a specific web page should appear in the text in that page. Be careful, however, not to overload pages with keywords. Aim for an appropriate keyword density to achieve optimal results.

Keyword density measures the ratio of a selected keyword to the rest of the words on a website page. For example, if a keyword you've selected for a particular page is "parasailing" and you use "parasailing" five times in a 120-word page, then your keyword density is approximately 4 percent.

You should aim for a keyword density between 2 percent and 5 percent. This is a case where more isn't necessarily better. If you stuff web pages with keywords, you can be penalized for keyword spamming and defeat the purpose of using keywords in the first place.

In addition to including your keywords in regular text, you should also use keywords in headings, such as H1 and H2 tags, and linked text.

Tip	Many people are tempted to use text, such as "click here" or "learn more" in their linked text, but you miss an SEO opportunity by doing so. Instead, use descriptive content in your links, particularly content that includes your keywords. For example, let's say you want someone to click a link to read your content on puppy training. Your link should say "puppy training tips" or "read more on puppy training," not just "read more."

To measure the keyword density of a published web page, try these free tools:

- Keyword Density Analyzer (**www.keyworddensity.com**)
- Webjectives Keyword Density Analyzer (**www.webjectives.com/keyword.htm**)

Tip	For additional features and more complex analysis, consider purchasing SEO software such as WebPosition Gold (**www.web-positiongold.com**), which offers both standard and professional versions.

Optimizing Meta Tags

Meta tags are informational tags that appear in the head section of your web page's HTML code. Search engines can use the information in these tags to describe your site in their search results.

Here's an example of meta tag use in the HTML code of a web page:

```
<HEAD>

<title>Yoga: A Five Minute Guide</title>

<meta name="description" content="Yoga web resources, books, and DVDs">

<meta name="keywords" content="yoga resources, yoga book re-views, yoga DVD reviews">

</HEAD>
```

To view meta tags on any web page, right-click the page from your browser. Then select View Source (Internet Explorer or Netscape) or View Page Source (Firefox). The source HTML appears, and you can analyze the use of meta tags on that page.

Tip	Don't worry. You don't need to be an HTML expert to add meta tags to your web pages. With most web design programs, it's easy to view and modify your HTML code. Just modify the sample text from this book to suit your own needs and enter in your HTML head section.

There are numerous meta tags, but the most common are:

- **Title tag.** The title tag isn't an official meta tag, but it's grouped with meta tags in the head section and is usually discussed in conjunction with meta tags. The text you enter in your title tag is what appears in a browser's title bar whenever someone views your page on the web. Your title tag should be no more than 60 characters and should optimally contain your most important keywords for that page as well as your name, your book's name, or your company name, depending on the focus of your site.
- **Description tag.** Some search engines use the text in your description tag to describe your page in search results. Others use text from the body of your web page or create their own description. Try to create a description tag with no more than 250 characters.
- **Keywords tag.** The keywords tag enables you to list the keywords for this page. Many search engines now ignore the keywords meta tag, but it doesn't hurt to include your keywords. Aim for a keywords tag with no more than 1,024 characters.

- **Robots tag.** This tag is useful for pages that you do *not* want search engines to crawl. The structure is: <meta name="robots" content="noindex,nofollow">. You generally want search engines to find all of the pages on your site, but you could want to avoid confirmation or thank-you pages as well as pages on which you deliver special reports or digital downloads to your customers.

Web-Savvy in Action

Rudy is the author of a book on healthcare public relations and is the president of a healthcare PR firm, RDW Communications. When creating his page titles and meta tags, he decides to focus both on his company name and on his target keyword phrase of "healthcare public relations."

```
<HEAD>
<title> Healthcare public relations by RDW
Communications
</title>
<meta name="description" content="RDW Communi-
cations offers strategic healthcare public re-
lations and marketing services">
<meta name="keywords" content="healthcare pub-
lic relations, RDW communications, Boston,
PRSA APR">
</HEAD>
```

Even though not all search engines use them, Rudy also decides to add more information in the keywords meta tag, such as the fact that he's located in Boston and he holds the APR designation from the Public Relations Society of America.

Describing Your Site Images with ALT Tags

An ALT tag is an HTML tag that displays alternative text when an image doesn't display on your website. ALT tags improve site navigation, assist visitors with slow Internet connections, and enhance site accessibility for disabled visitors.

In addition, ALT tags that include your targeted keywords can also improve your search engine visibility. This is particularly important if you use images to display content or as a navigational tool. Without the ALT tag, search engines may overlook important content when indexing your site.

Most web design programs enable you to easily add ALT tags to your images. You can also include this information directly in your HTML code such as in this example:

```
<img border="2" src="images/patrice.jpg" width="128"
height="130" alt="Patrice-Anne Rutledge Author Photo">
```

Creating a Sitemap

To ensure that all of the pages in your site are indexed, include a sitemap. A simple sitemap includes links to all of the pages on your site, categorized by topic. In many cases, your web design software can help you create a sitemap. Be sure to include a link to your sitemap page from your home page. Your bottom navigation bar is a good place for this link.

If you want to improve your ranking on Google, also consider Google Sitemaps (**www.google.com/webmasters/sitemaps**). Google Sitemaps is a free feature that helps Google find more pages on your site and enables you to view site statistics.

In order to use the Google Sitemap Generator script, you must be able to run scripts on your web server with Python 2.2 or later. If this sounds too complicated, check out these third-party tools that create a sitemap by simply entering your site URL:

- Free Sitemap Generator (**www.freesitemapgenerator.com**)
- Google Sitemap Creator (**www.pingoat.com/goat/google_sitemap**)
- XML Sitemap Generator (**www.xml-sitemaps.com**)

Linking to Your Site

Having other sites, particularly high-traffic sites, link to your website can increase your search engine ranking. Here are some tips for getting quality sites to link to you by using your keywords:

- Search on your target keywords to find the sites that rank highest for these terms. Contact the sites that aren't direct competitors and ask to exchange links.
- Find out who links to your major competitors and ask them to exchange links. To determine which sites link to your competitors, do some competitive intelligence on a link popularity site such as LinkPopularity.com (**www.linkpopularity.com**).
- Create a special "Link to This Site" page or section in which you offer sample text for others wanting to link to you. The link text you provide can describe your site exactly as you want it to be described, using your target keywords. If you contact other sites directly regarding a link exchange, include your link text in your email.

Web-Savvy in Action

Bianca is a food writer who specializes in organic cooking. She's written three books on this topic, owns a catering company specializing in organic foods, and frequently teaches cooking workshops. The keyword phrase she's targeting is "organic cooking." She offers to exchange reciprocal links with related websites and provides text to use for links to her site, "Organic Cooking by Bianca—Books, Catering, and Cooking Workshops."

Avoiding Broken Links

Broken links are bad news. Not only do they make a poor impression on your site visitors, but they also can make it difficult for search engines to index your site properly.

Many web design programs have utilities for locating broken links. You can also use a free utility to test for broken links in your site, such as Dead-Links.com (**www.dead-links.com**), or a comprehensive fee-based website management tool, such as NetMechanic (**www.netmechanic.com**).

Don't Be Invisible

Avoid using hidden text or links, such as making the font color of extraneous keywords the same color as your background text in the hope that it will help your search engine ranking. It won't. If you want to rank highly for the keyword "spelunking," then create quality content about spelunking. Don't enter this keyword forty times on a page in a font color that makes it invisible.

Submitting Your Site

The good news on search engine submission is that the majority of your traffic will come from just a few search engines. When I recently checked my website logs for one of my book companion sites, I discovered that more than 80 percent of my traffic came from Google, Yahoo!, and Live Search, with Google clearly providing the greatest traffic.

The remaining traffic came from a wide variety of lesser-known sources, each contributing less than two percent. So, instead of trying to get listed in hundreds of search engines, focus on getting a good ranking on the ones that drive the most traffic.

Because it takes time for your site to be spidered, you should submit as soon it's live on the web. If your site is just a shell and isn't ready for prime time, however, you're better off waiting to go live until your site is complete.

Submitting Your Site to Major Search Engines

Here are the URLs for submitting your site for free to major search engines:

- Google (**www.google.com/addurl.html**)
- Live Search (**search.msn.com/docs/submit.aspx**)
- Yahoo! (**search.yahoo.com/info/submit.html**)

Be sure to read the guidelines available on each site for successful site submission. Google, for example, offers tips at **www.google.com/webmasters/guidelines.html**.

Tip	You can also submit your site to the Yahoo! Directory for a review fee. If your site is accepted, you must pay the fee on an annual basis to remain in the directory. If you're on a tight budget, try the free submission first. Analyze your results before paying to be included in the directory.

Submitting to the Open Directory Project

The Open Directory Project (**www.dmoz.org**) is a large web directory run by a team of more than 70,000 volunteer editors. The advantage of a listing in the ODP is that its content is available in search results on AOL Search, Netscape Search, Lycos, HotBot, and many other portals and search engines. To submit your URL, first choose the appropriate category. Then click the "Suggest URL" link on that page.

Speeding Up the Process by Linking from Your Other Sites

One easy way to speed up the process of getting listed in search engine results is to include a link to your new website from your blog or another existing site that's already been spidered by search engines. I followed this plan with my latest book companion site, linking to it from both my main author site and my blog. My new site appeared on Yahoo!, Google, and Live Search very quickly.

Moreover, this was without manually submitting my site to any of these search engines. A listing is just the first step, though. Getting good keyword results takes time and patience.

Tip	You may have seen services offering to submit your site to hundreds of search engines for a fee. Although using a service such as this doesn't hurt, it's usually more cost-effective to submit for free to the major search engines. Save your SEO budget for PPC or other campaigns that will generate better results than paying for submission to a large number of search engines few people may use to find your site.

Piggybacking on the Search Engine Success of Others

If you don't have another website or blog from which to link to your new site, get other sites to link to you. While you're waiting for your site to rise in the search engine rankings, piggyback on the success of others by getting high-ranking sites to mention you.

To utilize this technique, do a search on your favorite search engine for your target keywords. Make a list of the sites ranking in the top 20 that complement your site and aren't direct competitors. Visit these sites to see how you could contribute to them. For example, you could:

- Ask to exchange links

- Enter relevant comments if the site is a blog
- Participate in message board conversations, if applicable
- Submit articles
- Request a review of your book
- Include the site on your virtual book tour

▶ See chapter 12, "Promoting Your Book with Article Marketing"

▶ See chapter 13, "Promoting Your Book with a Virtual Book Tour"

Web-Savvy in Action

Gus just wrote what he considers the definitive guide to snorkeling in the Caribbean. He creates a website for his book, but, so far, it hasn't received much traffic. Gus does a search on his primary keyword phrase to see which sites rank the highest for it. The first five sites listed include:

- A Caribbean travel site
- A snorkeling site
- The site of a direct competitor; another snorkeling author
- A small specialty site on Caribbean snorkeling
- A brochure-style site for a company that arranges snorkeling trips on a specific Caribbean island

Gus contacts the sites that aren't direct competitors and arranges several link exchanges and article contributions. He also starts participating on the message board of the snorkeling site, offering solid snorkeling advice and letting his signature file do the "selling" for him.

Tracking Your Site's Success

After optimizing your site and submitting it to selected search engines, start tracking results.

Analyzing Your Site Statistics

Most web hosts provide statistics that give you detailed information on your site visitors, the keywords they used to find your site, who is reaching your site through links, and much more. Keep in mind that it may take a couple months to generate meaningful site data.

Determining Your Link Popularity

On the web, just as in life, popularity counts. Here are two tools that analyze your link popularity and determine which sites link to you:

- **LinkPopularity.com (www.linkpopularity.com)**. Analyzes your link popularity on Google, Yahoo!, and MSN/Live Search. Also offers quality information on how to increase your link popularity.
- **Marketleap Link Popularity Check (www.marketleap.com/publinkpop)**. Enables you to compare your link popularity with up to three other sites. Also offers other search engine marketing tools.

Verifying Your Rankings

You should regularly verify your ranking on key search engines. Do this manually by entering your keywords in a specific search engine and to see where your site ranks. Alternatively, use an online tool to display this information. Some tools to try include:

- **Alexa (www.alexa.com)**. Offers the free Alexa toolbar, from which you can view traffic rank and link information on all of the sites you visit. You can also check a specific site's traffic rankings directly from the Alexa site without the toolbar.
- **Google Rankings (www.googlerankings.com)**. Displays your search ranking on Google, as well as Yahoo! and Live Search, for a specific keyword or keyword phrase. You need a Google API key to use this service, which you can get free when you sign up for a Google account. Google Rankings is an independent site not affiliated with Google.
- **Google Toolbar (toolbar.google.com)**. Enables you to view the Google PageRank of the sites you visit. PageRank is a number between 1 and 10 that indicates the relative importance of a web page as determined by the number of incoming links from other high-quality sites, among other things. The Google toolbar also offers a variety of other useful tools including a Google search box, word translator, and automated online maps linked to physical addresses mentioned on the web.
- **MyGoogle PageRank (www.mygooglepagerank.com)**. Displays a site's Google PageRank without installing the Google toolbar. This site is an independent site not affiliated with Google.

Reevaluating Your Plan

Search engine optimization isn't a one-time project. You should regularly analyze your results, study your competitors, and adjust your own site as needed. Be sure to keep your idea of search engine success in perspective. A site that focuses on a specialized niche will never achieve the same results as a site with more broad general appeal. The best way to analyze your success is to compare how you rank related to your direct competitors.

Search Engine Optimization Step-by-Step

Proper search engine optimization (SEO) can generate lots of traffic to your website. Here's your step-by-step "to do" list:

- ☐ Research SEO and verify that you understand the basic concepts
- ☐ Research and select keywords that relate directly to your goals and target audience
- ☐ Optimize your site content, including headings, with keywords
- ☐ Optimize meta tags such as the title, description, and keywords tags
- ☐ Generate a sitemap
- ☐ Create a plan to increase the number of links to your site through a natural, not artificial, process
- ☐ Submit your site to search engines and directories
- ☐ Analyze your site statistics regularly and revise your SEO techniques accordingly

3

Promoting Your Book with a Blog

Do you have a blog to promote your book? If not, get one. Whether you write fiction or nonfiction, a blog can help you develop and communicate with an audience for your writing. A blog is a powerful online marketing tool, and you should make the most of it. Another advantage is that it's far easier to get a simple blog up and running than it is to create a complex website.

Blogging 101

Are the terms weblog, blogosphere, blogrolling, and vlogging new to you? Read on to get the scoop on the basics of blogging.

Blogging Basics

Before you create your own blog, you need to understand a bit about blogging. The term "blog" is short for weblog, an online journal whose main content consists of dated journal entries. Although blogs may have started out primarily as personal journals, business blogging has become more common as savvy business owners realize that the personal touch a blog provides is a good way to market their products to an interested audience.

A blog may look like a website at first glance, but its format, content, and tone are decidedly unique. Most blogs include a main column with dated journal entries surrounded by either one or two sidebars, which contain additional information. The content of your blog entries should relate to the theme of your blog, but you can write in a far more casual tone than typical business communications. Think of each blog entry as a "from me to you" communication to your target audience. Blogs are personality driven. Make sure that your personality is easily identified in your blog content.

Tip	By using your blogging tool's "page" feature, it's becoming increasingly popular to combine your website and blog into a single online presence.

The world of blogging has its own set of terminology. Here are the most common terms:

- **Audioblog** - a blog that consists primarily of audio posts
- **Blogger** - a person who blogs
- **Blogosphere** - the totality of all blogs on the web
- **Blogroll** - a list of blogs you read and recommend, often displayed in a blog sidebar
- **Blogstorm** - extensive blog coverage on a particular hot topic
- **Moblog** - a mobile blog, in which blog posts come from a mobile phone or PDA
- **Permalink** - a static address for a blog posting
- **Photoblog** - a blog that consists primarily of photos
- **Ping** - notifying web directories and search engines that a blog has new content
- **Trackback** - a feature enabling you to notify another blog that you linked to one of its posts, in return receiving a link back to your blog
- **Vlog** - a video blog in which blog posts are primarily in a video format

Tip	As blogging evolves, more and more blogs are taking advantage of audio, images, video, and mobile posting, diminishing the need for terms like audioblog, photoblog, vlog, and moblog. However, it's still good to know what these terms mean if you hear them.

Don't let this long list daunt you. Despite its unique terminology, basic blogging really isn't that difficult.

Exploring the Blogosphere

If you're not very familiar with blogs, get started by exploring the blogosphere. One blog you should visit regularly is The Web-Savvy Writer Blog (**www.websavvywriter.com**), a blog companion to this book.

Also, search blog directories to find interesting blogs. Some good directories to try include:

- BlogCatalog (**www.blogcatalog.com**)
- Google Blog Search (**blogsearch.google.com**)
- Technorati (**www.technorati.com**)

Tip	If you find a variety of interesting blogs to read, bookmark them just as you would any other website. Alternatively, subscribe to blog feeds or to blog email updates, described later in this chapter.

Checking Out the Competition

While surveying the blogosphere, you should pay particular attention to your competitors' blogs. Viewing the blogs of other authors can give you ideas on what you want to include—and not include—on your own blog.

Creating a Blogging Plan

Before creating your blog, you need a plan. It doesn't have to be fancy or complex, but you should have distinct goals in mind before you start your blogging adventure. Ask yourself the following questions:

- **Who is my audience?** Are you trying to reach mystery fans, travelers to the American Southwest, new parents, or potential clients for services related to your book? Decide who you want to reach and what content would interest them.
- **What response do I want from my audience?** Do you want them to buy your books, hire you for consulting assignments, sign up for your seminars, or buy your audio CDs and special reports? What blog content supports these goals?
- **What keywords would my audience use in a search engine to find the information they seek?** For example, would your audience search for "parenting tips," "New Mexico travel," or "small business consulting"? Do some keyword research first. Then keep your target keywords in mind as you create your blog content.

▸ See chapter 2, "Promoting Your Book with SEO," Optimizing Your Content with Keywords

Creating Your Blog

With a plan in place, it's time to create your blog.

Choosing a Blogging Tool

One of your most important decisions is the selection of a blogging tool. There are essentially two options for setting up your blog: a hosted blogging service or blog software that you download and configure. Some blogging tools to consider include:

- **Blogger (www.blogger.com).** Blogger is a hosted blogging service that's easy to use. Because it's hosted, you don't need to have an existing website or use any special software to create your blog. Just log in from any computer and blog away. One of the biggest advantages of Blogger, which Google owns, is that it's free. On the downside, Blogger doesn't enable you to create static pages on your blog. You also need to use a third-party tool to utilize trackbacks.

- **TypePad** (www.typepad.com). TypePad is a hosted blogging service that offers the ability to create static pages and utilize trackbacks, which makes it popular with business bloggers. TypePad offers three levels of service with varied monthly fees. Depending on the level you choose, additional features include the ability to create multiple blogs, blog with multiple authors, schedule your posts, customize your blog design, and map to a domain (**www.websavvywriter.com** instead of **websavvywriterblog.typepad.com**, for example). If you want to see if TypePad is the right tool for you, sign up for a free 30-day trial.

- **WordPress.com** (www.wordpress.com). WordPress.com is a free, hosted blogging solution that offers a long list of features including the ability to create static pages, view statistics, and more. There is a small annual fee, however, if you want to map your blog to a domain or modify your theme's layout and fonts.

- **WordPress.org** (www.wordpress.org). WordPress.org is similar to the hosted WordPress.com, but is software that you host on your own server. The advantages of installing your own version of WordPress are that it's free and filled with more features than the hosted version of WordPress. The main disadvantage is that it requires more technical skill to set up than a hosted solution. Many web hosts offer easy WordPress installation through the Fantasico installer, however. Host Gator (**www.hostgator.com**) is a good web hosting choice if you're interested in installing WordPress.

Making the Most of Sidebars

Most blogs are designed with a large center column and two sidebars, although some bloggers choose to only use one sidebar. Your center column contains your blog postings. You're free to add your own content to the sidebars. Here are some suggestions for good sidebar content:

- Background information
  Include a brief bio or a link to a more detailed bio. Be sure to include your name if it isn't in your blog title or tagline. Blogs are a highly personal form of communication and your audience needs to know who you are and connect with you.

- Your photo
  Posting a photo on your blog helps to personalize it. Because of its heritage as a journaling mechanism, blogging has a "from me to you" mentality.

- Information about your books and other products and services

You need to let your blog readers know who you are and what you do, but it's important not to oversell on a blog. A blog isn't a sales brochure; it's a communication vehicle.

- Category listings
  Categorizing your posts makes it easier for visitors to find the information they're seeking, particularly if you have many blog postings.

- Lists of books you have written or recommend
  TypePad offers an automated way to do this and easily enables you to include your Amazon Associates ID in these links.

- Context-sensitive ads
  Good options include Google AdSense or Yahoo! Publisher Network. Be careful not to overdo advertising on your blog. Ads may work on a topic-focused blog, but they aren't always a good idea on an author-focused blog.

- Feed subscription link
  Offering information on how to subscribe to your blog's feed, including buttons for the most common readers, increases the likelihood of casual readers becoming subscribers.

- A sign-up link for your ezine
- Links to your website and other related sites
- A blogroll, or list of other blogs you read

▶ See chapter 6, "Promoting Your Book with an Ezine"

▶ See chapter 8, "Selling and Promoting Your Book on Amazon.com," Making Money with Amazon Associates

▶ See chapter 9, "Promoting Your Book with Online Advertising," Generating Advertising Revenue

Adding Meaningful Content

Regularly adding meaningful content is difficult for many people. Here are 15 good content ideas for your blog:

1. Offer tips and suggestions that your readers can actually use

2. Link to articles you've recently written

3. Comment on a newsworthy event related to you blog topic

4. Provide insight on industry events

5. Solicit reader tips and suggestions

6. Respond to blog comments

7. Post links to your recent interviews

8. Interview a non-competing expert

9. Share resources and information

10. Comment on other interesting sites and blogs

11. Recommend non-competing books, publications, and websites that are useful to your audience

12. Report live from tradeshows and other industry events

13. Report live from your travels

14. Tell a story that is relevant to your audience

15. Let a guest author post entries on your blog

Tip	Adding audio, video, and images to your blog can help your blog stand out from the crowd and attract more visitors.

▶ See chapter 5, "Promoting Your Book with a Podcast"

▶ See chapter 10, "Promoting Your Book with Audio and Video"

Creating Blog Content with Keywords in Mind

Although your blog content should never be contrived to suit keywords, you should keep your blog keywords in mind every time you write a post. Including relevant keywords in your blog headings, content, and linked text helps with search engine rankings.

Tip	Many of the search engine optimization tips that apply to websites also apply to blogs. Review chapter 2 for more ideas on utilizing keywords in your blog and optimizing your blog for search engines.

▶ See chapter 2, "Promoting Your Book with SEO"

Hosting Your Blog on Its Own Domain

Although it's not a requirement, you should consider hosting your blog on its own domain (**www.mybookblog.com**) or as an extension to your main author or book website (**www.mywebsite.com/blog**). To do this, register the domain name you want for your blog. Then map to this domain from your blogging tool. For example, the blog companion to this book is located at **www.websavvywriter.com**. If I didn't host it on its own domain, its URL could be **websavvywriter.blogspot.com** or **websavvywriter.typepad.com**. Blogger, TypePad, and WordPress all enable you to map your blog to its own domain.

Web-Savvy in Action	Ashleigh is a young novelist and the author of a humorous book for teenage girls. After signing on to write several more books, she decides to create a blog to develop a following for her series. Ashleigh's blog is very personality-driven and interactive. She encourages girls to comment on her blog and write to her with questions that she answers in future postings. Although Ashleigh does include an Amazon Associates link to her book and a few affiliate links in her sidebar, the focus of her blog is less on commerce and more on developing popularity and credibility with her target audience.

Making Money with Your Blog

Although most bloggers profit from their blog indirectly, making money is also possible through the selective use of advertising, affiliate links, and donation requests.

Accepting Advertising on Your Blog

Placing ads on your blog won't really help you market your books, but it can often help defray the cost of any blog hosting expenses. Some advertising options to consider include:

- AdBrite (**www.adbrite.com**)
- BlogAds (**www.blogads.com**)
- BlogKits (**www.blogkits.com**)
- Chitika (**www.chitika.com**)
- CrispAds (**www.crispads.com**)
- Google AdSense (**www.google.com/adsense**)
- Kanoodle BrightAds (**www.kanoodle.com**)
- Yahoo! Publisher Network (**publisher.yahoo.com**)

▸ See chapter 9, "Promoting Your Book with Online Advertising," Generating Advertising Revenue

Asking for Donations

Another way to make money from your blog is to simply ask for it. Although not suitable for every blog, consider placing a donation button on your blog if you feel the information you provide would motivate your audience to offer a donation. Here are several options:

- Amazon Honor System (**www.amazon.com/honorsystem**)
- PayPal donation button (**www.paypal.com**)
- TypePad tip jar, with a Pro account (**www.typepad.com**)

Placing Affiliate Links on Your Blog

You can make some extra money by recommending carefully selected products for your blog visitors to purchase. Find interesting products to recommend through any of the following affiliate programs:

- Amazon Associates (**www.amazon.com/associates**)
- Commission Junction (**www.cj.com**)
- LinkShare (**www.linkshare.com**)

Here are some tips on making the most of affiliate links:

- Choose products that directly relate to the subject of your blog, preferably those that you have actually used and strongly recommend.
- Place banner ads from your affiliates on your blog sidebars, if you're willing to have the appearance of an advertising-supported blog.
- Create a blog post describing your personal experience with an affiliate product. Include the affiliate link in this post.
- Describe books you've written, or would recommend. Include your Amazon Associates ID in the link to the Amazon web page for each book.
- Be careful not to let affiliate offerings detract from your own products and services.

Web-Savvy in Action	Travis is a personal trainer and the author of a book on fitness for the time-challenged. Travis posts three blog entries a week—written in a friendly, casual tone—which has helped to cement his reputation as both a fitness expert and someone who's open and accessible to his audience. He's currently planning a "spring into fitness" feature for April, in which he'll include a fitness plan for each day of that month. Travis also encourages reader comments and regularly replies to them. In order to generate additional income, Travis uses his sidebars to display Amazon Associates links to his fitness book, affiliate links to products he personally recommends, and supplemental advertising.

▶ See chapter 8, "Selling and Promoting Your Book on Amazon.com," Making Money with Amazon Associates

▶ See chapter 9, "Promoting Your Book with Online Advertising," Generating Advertising Revenue

Getting Your Blog Noticed

You could have the most informative, well-written blog in your particular niche, but, if no one is reading it, it won't benefit you. Here are some ideas to get the traffic flowing.

Blogging Frequently

A blog is not a static website. If you create a blog, post a few entries, and leave it sit there for several weeks, you're defeating the purpose of creating your blog in the first place. Your audience won't return to a blog that isn't current and you won't get the attention of search engines with stale content either.

Set a blogging schedule (preferably, at least two or three times a week) and stick to it. If blogging several times a week is difficult, then set aside several hours to create all of your blog entries for a set period of time, such as a week or month. Save them as drafts and then publish based on your schedule.

Submitting to Search Engines and Directories

Now that you have this really cool blog, it's time to let the world know about it. You should submit your blog to search engines, just as you would any other website. Chapter 2 covers search engine submission, but, as a reminder, here's a list of the most popular engines and directories to which you should submit:

- Google (**www.google.com/addurl.html**)
- Live Search (**search.msn.com/docs/submit.aspx**)
- Open Project Directory (**www.dmoz.com**)
- Yahoo! (**search.yahoo.com/info/submit.html**)

Tip   Although being listed in the major search engines should generate most of your search-related blog traffic, you can also submit to blog-specific search engines such as Google Blog Search (**blogsearch.google.com**) or BlogCatalog (**www.blogcatalog.com**).

▶ See chapter 2, "Promoting Your Book with SEO," Submitting Your Site

Creating a Blog Feed

A blog feed, frequently referred to as an RSS feed, is a document that contains summaries of your blog posts, to which people can subscribe and read with a feed reader. This is particularly useful for those who follow numerous blogs and don't want to visit each blog site to read the latest postings. You should definitely create a feed for your blog. Chapter 4 offers complete details on how to do this.

▶ See chapter 4, "Promoting Your Book with a Feed"

Pinging Blog Services

When you update your blog, use a ping utility to notify multiple blog update services that you have new blog content. Using a utility to notify multiple services—such as Technorati, My Yahoo!, and Moreover—with a single entry is a big timesaver. Pinging helps to index your blog faster, which leads to greater search engine visibility. Some free ping utilities to consider include:

- King Ping (**www.kping.com**)
- Pingoat (**www.pingoat.com**)
- Ping-O-Matic (**www.pingomatic.com**)

If you use FeedBurner (**www.feedburner.com**) to create a feed for your blog, you can ping up to 10 services automatically.

▶ See chapter 4, "Promoting Your Book with a Feed," Creating a Feed with FeedBurner

Tip	Technorati (**www.technorati.com**) is a blog search engine that all three ping utilities update. Consider registering your blog with Technorati to utilize its tagging functionality, which can help increase your blog traffic.

Ping utilities notify many of the same services. It isn't necessary, or even advisable, to ping the same sites multiple times. Don't overdo pinging. Ping once when you have updated content, and that's it.

Creating Trackbacks to Other Blog Posts

A trackback enables you to notify another blog that you have referenced one of its posts. A link back to your blog appears on the referenced blog, which can help generate more traffic to your blog.

SixApart, the company that created the TypePad blogging service, first introduced the trackback concept, which is now also available with many other blogging tools such as WordPress, B2, Nucleus, and Bloxsom. Blogger currently does not support trackbacks, but it offers backlink functionality instead. If you want to use trackbacks with Blogger, use an external service such as HaloScan (**www.haloscan.com**).

Commenting on Other Blogs

Find other blogs that your target audience might read and comment on interesting blog posts. Entering a blog comment is easy. Most blogs have a link next to each post that you can click to open a comment page or dialog box where you can enter a comment.

Adding insightful commentary or other useful information is far more helpful than just indicating that you like—or dislike—a specific post. By listing your name and the URL of your blog, people will come and check you out if they feel your comment adds value.

Promoting Your Blog Everywhere

Promote your blog by including its URL on your:

- Website
- Ezine
- Other blogs
- Email signature file
- Autoresponder content
- Printed material

Offering an Email Subscription to Your Blog

Offering an email subscription service for your blog can help you drive additional traffic. Some readers may view your blog directly. Others may subscribe to your feed. Offering email updates provides yet another way to keep in touch with your audience, one that may already be very familiar to readers who don't use feeds or are put off by any complex-sounding technology.

Two services to check out include FeedBlitz (**www.feedblitz.com**) and Zookoda (**www.zookoda.com**). FeedBurner (**www.feedburner.com**) offers its own email subscription service as well as provides built-in support for FeedBlitz.

▶ See chapter 4, "Promoting Your Book with a Feed"

Creating a Blogroll

You can create a blogroll, a list of other blogs that you read, and post it on your blog for your audience to see. Both BlogRolling (**www.blogrolling.com**) and Bloglines (**www.bloglines.com**) enable you to create blogrolls. A blogroll is advantageous because it encourages others to link back to you, which can potentially enhance your search engine ranking and increase your readership.

Tracking Your Blog's Stats

To validate the effectiveness of your blog and your blog marketing efforts, you need to view detailed statistics about your blog traffic. One great tool to consider is MyBlogLog (**www.mybloglog.com**).

Tip	Also, consider tracking your blog with Google Analytics (**www.google.com/analytics**).

New Trends in Blogging

Already tired of your basic blog? Here are more ideas using the latest blogging trends.

Blooks

The precise definition of a blook varies, but it's derived from the words blog and book. In some cases, it refers to a book that is delivered via a blog, with each chapter a separate blog post. A blook can also refer to a print book derived from blog content. If you're interested in the concept of a blook, take a look at **www.hackoff.com**, an Internet murder mystery by Tom Evslin that's a classic example of a book serialized on a blog.

Web-Savvy in Action	Hilda and Ingrid—a pair of adventurous, twentysomething sisters—spent the past year sailing around the world, documenting their travels in a blog. Their blog, filled with colorful descriptions and photos of exotic locales, drew a large audience.
	Now the sisters have decided to create a book based on their blog—in essence, a blook. Their plan is to rework their blog content into a chapter-based book, self-publish it, and promote it across the Internet, where they have already achieved a great deal of publicity.

Mobile Blogging

A mobile blog, also known as a moblog, is a blog with extensive entries (text, photo, or video) sent to your blog by cell phone or PDA. This is useful if you frequently blog on the road and want to share your experiences with your audience.

Many blogging tools already have some mobile blogging functionality. Here are two other resources to consider:

- **Flickr (www.flickr.com)**. Enables you to take photos with your cell phone and post to blogs created with tools such as Blogger, TypePad, and WordPress.
- **Nokia Lifeblog (europe.nokia.com/lifeblog)**. Publishes images, video, messages, and notes from your Nokia phone to your TypePad account.

Blogmapping

If you're interested in displaying a map of the location from which you blog, consider adding a blog map to your site. This is probably a fun extra for most bloggers, but, if you blog from multiple locations or want to map a travel-related blog, blogmapping may interest you and your blog audience. Some choices to consider include:

- **FeedMap** (**www.feedmap.net**). Uses Microsoft MapPoint technology to create a BlogMap that you can place on your blog.
- **Frappr!** (**www.frappr.com**). Enables you to create a map showing the locations of a group of users, such as your blog visitors, readers, and subscribers.

Web-Savvy in Action

Raley is a tour guide and the author of several guidebooks to New Zealand. He's also a technology buff who's eager to try out the latest in blogging technologies. He creates a blog that follows him on a one-month adventure tour of New Zealand, providing a multimedia showcase of everything his country has to offer.

His posts include a mixture of photos, video, and audio content, delivered via his cell phone, digital camera, and notebook computer. Raley also posts a map detailing the route of his travels.

Blogging Step-by-Step

Setting up a basic blog can be a fast and easy task. Keep in mind, though, that a blog isn't static and requires ongoing content to be successful. Here's your step-by-step "to do" list:

- ☐ Research blogging and verify that you understand the basic concepts
- ☐ View competitive blogs to get an idea of what works and what doesn't
- ☐ Choose the blogging tool that's right for you and sign up for that service or install the appropriate software on your server
- ☐ Customize your blog template, images, and sidebars to suit your needs and individual personality
- ☐ Start adding content (and more content and more content)
- ☐ Use your keywords in your blog posts when appropriate
- ☐ Notify ping services when you post new content (many blogging tools, as well as FeedBurner, do this for you automatically)
- ☐ Consider including advertising on your blog if appropriate
- ☐ Sign up with a blog email subscription service (most are free) to give your readers another way to read your content
- ☐ Track your blog statistics, review your stats regularly, and adjust your format and content accordingly
- ☐ Promote your blog—on your website, on the web, and in search engines
- ☐ Research advanced blogging concepts such as photoblogging, videoblogging, and mobile blogging and incorporate into your blog over time
- ☐ Read chapter 4 "Promoting Your Book with a Feed" to learn how to promote your blog with feeds

4

Promoting Your Book with a Feed

When you publish a blog, you hope readers return frequently for your latest updates. One way they can do this is to bookmark your site. Another way is to enable readers to subscribe to a feed of your blog's content. A blog feed, also referred to as an RSS feed, is a document that contains summaries of your blog posts, to which people can subscribe and read with a feed reader. This is particularly useful for those who follow numerous blogs and don't want to visit each blog site to read the latest postings.

Although feeds are most commonly associated with blogs, you can also create a feed for a podcast or for website content. In this chapter, we'll focus on blog feeds.

Quick Fact	One in ten blog readers uses a feed reader to sort through the increasing number of published blogs available. *—Source: Nielsen//NetRatings*

Feeds 101

Before you create a feed for your blog, you need to understand the basics of how they work.

To better grasp the concept of a feed, look at the blog companion for this book, **www.websavvywriter.com**. In the right sidebar, click the orange and white feed icon. This opens a browser-friendly feed that I created using FeedBurner. On this page, you see a list of my recent blog posts as well as buttons for subscribing to my blog's feed. You'll learn how to subscribe to a feed, as well as create your own feed, later in this chapter.

▸ See "Creating a Feed with FeedBurner" in this chapter

Feed Technology

Creating, subscribing to, and reading a feed is a fairly simple process that requires limited technical skill. But in the early days, feeds were more the domain of technical users who talked about XML, RSS, and Atom. Although you don't need to know much about these technical terms to create a feed now, it doesn't hurt to understand what they mean if you come across them.

A feed is an XML-based document, which means that it uses Extensible Markup Language (XML) to format its contents. If you view the raw code of your feed, you'll see the XML, which looks something like HTML code. The two most popular feed formats are Atom and RSS, which stands for Really Simple Syndication.

Advantages of Feeds

Creating a feed has many advantages. With a feed, you can:

- Increase website traffic
- Enable readers to receive the latest updates to your blog, podcast, or website without remembering to visit your site
- Deliver information without worrying about getting blocked by a spam filter
- Attract users who don't like to subscribe to ezines, despite assurances of privacy
- Enable other publishers to syndicate your content
- Generate revenue by including advertising in your feeds

Feed Readers

In order to read a feed, you need access to a feed reader, also called an aggregator. There are essentially two types of feed readers: software that you download onto your own computer and web-based readers to which you log on from any computer. With a feed reader, you can read a feed as well as subscribe to it.

If you follow numerous blogs, being able to read updates in one location is a big timesaver. In addition to subscribing to blogs, you can also subscribe to podcasts, news (for example, the latest from CNN, the BBC, and the *New York Times*), and other feed content. Here are some popular free readers to check out:

- **Bloglines** (**www.bloglines.com**). Web-based reader offering email subscriptions and a mobile version for handheld computers and cell phones.
- **NewsGator** (**www.newsgator.com**). Offers a free web-based reader. For an added fee, you can access a mobile edition or an email edition.

- **Rojo (www.rojo.com)**. Web-based reader that also offers content tagging and social networking features.

If you already have an email or other account with Google, MSN, or Yahoo!, consider these additional reader options:

- **Google Reader (www.google.com/reader)**. Subscribe to feeds and other news using the familiar Google environment.
- **My MSN (my.msn.com)**. Add feeds as content modules on your My MSN page.
- **My Yahoo! (my.yahoo.com)**. Subscribe to feeds and display them on your My Yahoo! page.

Tip	Google Reader, My MSN, and My Yahoo! work best for subscribing to a small number of blog feeds.

Before creating your own feed, you should try out several feed readers and subscribe to a variety of feeds to get a feel for feeds in action.

Subscribing to Feeds

Although you can subscribe to feeds by searching for them on your favorite feed reader, you may often discover a blog you enjoy and want to subscribe directly from the blog itself. On many blogs, and websites as well, you'll see a variety of ways to subscribe to feeds:

- An orange button with white radio waves, now the industry standard
- Small buttons labeled RSS or XML
- Buttons for feed readers such as Bloglines or My Yahoo!
- Text links encouraging you to subscribe to the blog

Tip	Visit The Web-Savvy Writer book companion blog at **www.websavvywriter.com** to view an example of a feed subscription button.

Because there isn't one best way to subscribe to a feed, you'll see a variety of approaches on the blogs you read. Some bloggers include only one subscription button whereas others include a wide variety of alternatives. If you see a button for the feed reader you use, click the button to subscribe to the feed automatically.

Later in this chapter, you'll learn how to add feed subscription buttons to your own blog and website.

Creating Your Feed

Creating a feed for your blog is easy. In fact, most of the work is automatic.

Feed URLs

Your blogging tool will create your feed for you and provide you with its URL. You can use the feed as it is, or enhance it with a free service like FeedBurner. Here are some sample feed URLs:

- yourblog.blogspot.com/atom.xml
- yourblog.typepad.com/yourblog2/index.rdf
- yourblog.com/wp-rss.php

Be aware that the URL of your feed isn't the same as the URL of your blog itself. For example, the URL of the blog companion to this workbook is **www.websavvywriter.com**. Its feed is **feeds.feedburner.com/websavvywriter**, created with FeedBurner. Clicking a blog's URL takes you to the blog. Clicking a feed's URL lets you to subscribe to the feed.

Creating a Feed with FeedBurner

The feed your blogging tool generates will work just fine, but you might want to consider regenerating your feed using FeedBurner. There are many advantages to using FeedBurner. Some of the many features include the ability to:

- Generate a browser-friendly feed (no XML code appears when someone clicks your feed; instead, an easy-to-read instruction page appears)
- Republish your feed as HTML
- Automatically notify ping services when you update your blog, rather than having to do this manually
- Create interactive posts
- Offer email subscriptions to your blog
- Generate a variety of subscription buttons to place on your blog and website
- Insert your Amazon Associates ID into your feed (if someone buys a book you mention in your blog postings, you get a commission)
- Insert Google AdSense into your feed (text ads related to your feed content appear in your feed; you generate revenue when someone clicks an ad)
- View statistics on your site's circulation and readership

Tip   You can also offer email subscriptions to your blog with FeedBlitz (**www.feedblitz.com**).

▶ See chapter 3, "Promoting Your Book with a Blog," Offering an Email Subscription to Your Blog

FeedBurner includes step-by-step instructions for Blogger, TypePad, and WordPress users who want to create a FeedBurner feed. After creating your FeedBurner feed, use this URL instead of the URL your blogging tool generated.

▶ See chapter 8, "Selling and Promoting Your Book on Amazon.com"

▶ See chapter 9, "Promoting Your Book with Online Advertising"

Web-Savvy in Action

Ramona is a jazz musician and the author of several books on Brazilian jazz. She creates a blog to promote her books and music and would like to create a feed as well. Although the blogging tool she uses to publish her blog generates a feed, she decides to create an enhanced feed with FeedBurner. Her new feed is browser-friendly. When blog visitors click her feed link or button, a descriptive page appears telling them how to subscribe, instead of displaying a page of XML code.

In addition, Ramona notifies ping services of her new blog posts automatically so that she won't have to bother doing this herself whenever she has something new to say. Finally, Ramona activates the Amazon Associates and Google AdSense features so she can start making money from her feed.

Profiting from Your Feed

If you'd like to generate revenue from feed advertising, here are several options:

- **Feedburner (www.feedburner.com)**. Feedburner offers the FeedBurner Ad Network and Google AdSense for Content advertising options.
- **Google AdSense for Feeds (www.google.com/adsense)**. Currently in beta, AdSense for feeds enables you to display context-sensitive ads in your feeds, similar to how you would use AdSense on your blog or website.
- **Kanoodle (www.kanoodle.com)**. Place sponsored ads on your feed with the Kanoodle network.
- **Pheedo (www.pheedo.com)**. Another site that places ads in your feeds.
- **Yahoo! Publisher Network (publisher.yahoo.com)**. Yahoo! Publisher Network enables you to publish targeted ads in your feeds generated from WordPress or Moveable Type.

Some of your readers, however, could find feed advertising intrusive. Just like with your blog or website, you need to balance the income potential of advertising with its impact on your readers.

► See chapter 9, "Promoting Your Book with Online Advertising," Generating Advertising Revenue

Promoting Your Feed

Much of what you did to promote your blog also helps promote your feed, which is essentially a summary of your blog posts. There are several additional ways, however, to promote your feed.

Helping Google, Yahoo!, and My MSN Find Your Feed

Google, Yahoo!, and My MSN all have feed readers. By subscribing to your own feed through an account on these websites, their search engines have a better opportunity to track and index your feed. Google offers a personalized home page for users with a Google account. You can create a section that contains your feed on your Google home page.

Yahoo! makes it easy to promote your feed on Yahoo! with the information it provides in its Publisher's Guide to RSS (**publisher.yahoo.com/rssguide**).

Adding your feed as a content module on your My MSN page is equally simple through its Add Content feature.

Promoting Your Feed on Your Website and Blog

Once you have a feed, the first thing you should do is let your blog and website visitors know about it. One of the easiest ways to do this is to add feed subscription buttons, also referred to as chicklets, enabling your readers to subscribe to your blog feed.

To add these buttons, you need to generate HTML code that includes information about your feed and insert this code into your web page or blog. Don't worry, generating the HTML code is almost always an automated process. There are several ways to do this:

- If you use FeedBurner, click the Publicize tab and then the Chicklet Chooser button to generate the HTML code for the buttons you want to use. FeedBurner also enables you to use the feed icon that is becoming the industry standard (a small orange square with white radio waves).
- If you don't use FeedBurner, go to the websites of the feed readers whose buttons you want to add to your page (such as Bloglines, Rojo, My Yahoo!, and so forth) to find instructions on how to add their feed subscription buttons.
- If you use TypePad and don't want to bother with HTML code, you can easily enter a feed subscription text link in one of your sidebars.

Web-Savvy in Action

Rhoda is the author of a book on pet care who creates a blog companion to her book. To promote her blog further, she generates a feed. Rhoda feels that many of her target readers are unfamiliar with feeds, so she decides to educate her audience on their many advantages.

On the navigation bar on her website home page, she includes a text link for more information on her feed as well as a feed button that those familiar with the technology would recognize. Site visitors who click the text link transfer to a page in which she explains the basics of feeds, describes how they benefits readers, and offers multiple feed subscription buttons.

On her blog sidebar, Rhoda includes the same feed subscription buttons, a feed subscription text link, and a link to the page on her website in which she describes feeds. After providing this information, her feed subscriptions begin to increase dramatically.

Feeds Step-by-Step

Although the topic of feeds is probably one of the more complex technologies described in this book, creating a feed of your blog content can have a great payoff. Here's your step-by-step "to do" list:

- ☐ Research feed technology and verify that you understand the basic concepts
- ☐ Subscribe to several feeds to get a first-hand view of how it works
- ☐ Create your own feed with FeedBurner to take advantage of its advanced features (or use the feed your blogging tool provides if you prefer)
- ☐ Place feed subscription buttons on your blog to encourage subscribers
- ☐ Consider including advertising in your feed if you feel your subscriber volume warrants it
- ☐ Subscribe to your feed through Google, Yahoo!, and MSN for greater visibility
- ☐ Promote your feed in directories and on the web

5

Promoting Your Book with a Podcast

Think of a podcast as an Internet radio show you listen to on demand. The term podcast comes from the words iPod and broadcast. However, the iPod aspect of podcasting is misleading. You can listen to a podcast on an iPod, but listening on another media player or a computer capable of playing audio files works just as well.

With podcasting, the online audio content that you create is delivered via a feed. It's similar to your blog's feed, but it's for audio instead. Using the feed, listeners can "subscribe" to your podcast so they're aware of every new episode.

▶ See chapter 4, "Promoting Your Book with a Feed"
▶ See chapter 10, "Promoting Your Book with Audio and Video," Promoting with Audio

Quick Fact	Between 2004 and 2010, the use of podcasting among American consumers will enjoy an annual growth rate of 101 percent, approaching nearly 60 million people by 2010. *—Source: The Diffusion Group*

Podcasting 101

In order to determine whether podcasting is a good choice for your book promotion efforts, you need to learn the basics of podcasting.

Advantages of Podcasting

As an author, you can use podcasting to connect with your audience by:

- Telling a story
- Reading a book excerpt (serialized audio books are also called podiobooks)
- Delivering tutorials related to your area of expertise

- Producing your own talk show
- Providing audio travel content for travelers with an iPod or other MP3 player
- Offering paid subscriptions to value-added audio content

Tip	As an alternative to podcasting, consider hosting a blog talk radio show. Learn more at the BlogTalkRadio website (**www.blogtalkradio.com**).

Listening to Podcasts

Before creating your own podcast, you should listen to other podcasts to get a feel for what works well in this medium. There are several ways to listen to a podcast. You can:

- Listen directly from the web
- Download a podcast and listen to it later on your computer
- Download a podcast, transfer it to your digital audio player (such as an iPod or similar device), and listen to it whenever and wherever you want

When you find podcasts you like, you can subscribe to them just like you do with your favorite blog feeds. You can listen and subscribe to podcasts through a podcast reader, which is very similar to the feed readers you use to subscribe to blog feeds. In fact, many feed readers also enable you to subscribe to podcasts. Podcast readers are also called aggregators, podcast receivers, and podcatchers. Don't let all the terms confuse you. A podcast reader is essentially just software (or a website) that enables you to keep track of your favorite podcasts. Some podcast readers to check out include:

- **Doppler** (**www.dopplerradio.net**). Offers downloads of Doppler for Windows and DopplerMobile Beta.
- **iTunes** (**www.apple.com/itunes/podcasts**). With iTunes for Windows or the Mac, you can subscribe and listen to podcasts as well as take advantage of other iTunes music management features.
- **Juice** (**juicereceiver.sourceforge.net**). Juice, formerly known as iPodder, is available as a download for Windows and Mac platforms.
- **Yahoo! Podcasts** (**podcasts.yahoo.com**). Enables you to listen to podcasts directly from the web or subscribe and listen with either Yahoo! Music Engine or Apple iTunes. Also includes a podcast directory and information on podcasting.

Tip	If you'd like to listen to podcasts on your mobile phone, check out Mobilcast (**www.mobilcast.com**), which supports selected Nokia, Motorola, and Sony Ericcson phones. When you complete your own podcast, you can also add it to the directory.

Most podcast readers also offer podcast directories so you can search for interesting podcasts. Some book-related podcasts to check out include:

- Authors on Tour Live (**www.authorsontourlive.com**)
- Eye on Books Bookcast (**www.eyeonbooks.com/bookcast**)
- Holtzbrinck Publishers Podcast (**www.holtzbrinckpodcasts.com**)
- Podiobooks (**www.podiobooks.com**)
- Simon & Schuster SimonSays Podcast (**www.simonsays.com**)
- The Penguin Podcast (**thepenguinpodcast.blogs.com**)

Planning Your Podcast

In order to develop a podcasting plan, ask yourself the following questions:

- Who is your audience? What content do they want to listen to?
- What other podcasts target your same audience? How will your podcast differ?
- What is your podcast's goal? How does your content fit with that goal?
- What is your format? Will you be the sole speaker? Or will you interview others?
- How long will each podcast be?
- How frequently will you podcast? Monthly, weekly, or daily?

Web-Savvy in Action

Trevor is the self-published author of a mystery novel he has chosen to deliver as a podiobook, an audiobook delivered as a serialized podcast. He posts each chapter on his blog and also creates a podcast feed to promote his podiobook. His blog includes a link to Amazon.com, where listeners can purchase the print version of his book. A large graphic of the book's cover appears prominently on his blog.

Trevor isn't a well-known novelist, so he needs to promote his podiobook to develop an audience. He starts by contacting websites that target mystery buffs and then creates a series of online press releases related to his book. Because podiobooks are still a new concept, he's able to generate press coverage on his book and expand his audience.

Creating Your Podcast

There are several basics steps to creating a podcast:

- Record your podcast, either on your computer using recording software and a microphone or by phone
- Save your podcast as an MP3 file
- Upload your MP3 file to your server
- Create your podcast feed
- Publish and promote your feed

Don't worry if this sounds difficult to you. Many automated tools make podcasting easier.

▶ See chapter 4, "Promoting Your Book with a Feed"

Choosing Your Podcasting Tools and Technologies

If you plan to record your podcast on your computer, you'll need a good microphone and some basic recording software. Popular recording software programs to consider include:

- **Audacity** (**audacity.sourceforge.net**). Audacity is a free, open source software program for recording and editing sound. Popular with podcasters, it's available as a download for Windows, Mac, and Linux. If you need to export your sound file to an MP3 format (many podcast services do this for you, so it may not be necessary), you can download the optional LAME MP3 encoder to handle this task.
- **GarageBand** (**www.apple.com/ilife/garageband**). Apple's audio recording software for the Macintosh is particularly good for recording music, but also has many podcasting features. These include the ability to add a podcast artwork track, a built-in sound effects library, a speech enhancer, iChat interview recording, and one-click podcast publishing.

Don't plan to use the microphone that came with your computer, or your notebook's built-in microphone, for recording purposes. You need a solid, professional-quality microphone for high-quality podcasting. Plantronics, Behringer, and Stageworks all make affordable microphones that are suitable for author podcasts.

Creative Podcast Ideas

Here's a trio of ideas for those who want to create a more sophisticated podcast:

- **Add music to your podcast.** To do so, find royalty-free music suitable for podcasts, known as podsafe music. A good source to check out is the Podsafe Music Network (**music.podshow.com**).
- **Create a video podcast.** A video podcast is also referred to as a vidcast, vodcast, videocast, or vcast. Yes, the podcasting crowd does love catchy new names. This technique is similar to videoblogging, but it's delivered through a feed to which listeners can subscribe.
- **Include phone interviews in your podcast.** One service to consider is Conference Calls Unlimited (**www.conferencecallsunlimited.com**). Another option is to use the call recording features of Skype (**www.skype.com**) and Pamela for Skype (**www.pamela-systems.com**).

Web-Savvy in Action

Berrie is the author of a series of adventure travel guidebooks to the American Northwest. She likes the idea of creating a podcast to expand her audience and promote her books, but she wants to try something a little different.

Berrie enjoys making videos with her camcorder and creates a monthly video podcast that covers some of her favorite adventures in Washington, Oregon, and Idaho. She promotes her video podcast in podcast directories, on her website, and on other travel websites that are interested in both her content as well as the new podcast technology.

Hosting Your Podcast

Here are three podcast hosting options that make things easy for the novice podcaster:

- **Hipcast** (www.hipcast.com). Enables you to create your podcast in three ways: by telephone, through your web browser with a microphone and no additional software, or using audio software such as Audacity or GarageBand. You can incorporate your podcasts into your blogs hosted by Blogger, TypePad, WordPress, and other blogging tools. Hipcast is also compatible with FeedBurner and iTunes. Monthly fees vary based on storage requirements; bandwidth is unmetered. Offers free seven-day trial. Formerly called Audioblog.com.
- **Liberated Syndication** (www.libsyn.com). Offers four levels of podcast syndication services based on your storage requirements (from 100 megabytes to 800 megabytes). There is no charge for bandwidth usage. You can use their blogging interface or work with your own blogging tool.
- **Podblaze.com** (www.podblaze.com). Provides an easy-to-use podcast hosting service, including iTunes compatibility. Charges varied monthly fees based on storage and bandwidth requirements.

Tip

Looking for even more options? Consider Gabcast (**www.gabcast.com**), Odeo (**www.odeo.com**), or AudioAcrobat (**www.audioacrobat.com**).

PodPress (**www.podpress.org**) is a viable option for incorporating a podcast into a WordPress blog.

Creating a Podcast Feed with FeedBurner

In addition to generating a feed for your blog with FeedBurner (**www.feedburner.com**), you can also use FeedBurner to create a feed for your podcast. Although regenerating your feed with FeedBurner is optional, it does offer numerous worthwhile features that help you enhance, track, publicize, and make money with your feed.

Profiting from Your Podcast

Do you want to make some money from your podcast? New ways to profit from podcasting are just beginning to develop, but here are some ideas:

- Consider accepting advertising in your podcasts, also referred to as podvertising or advercasting
- Secure podcast sponsors related to your podcast topic
- Offer special discounts on your books, products, and services to your podcast listeners to generate more sales
- Discuss affiliate products that you recommend and refer listeners to your website for more information and related links
- Place ads, such as Google AdSense, on the web pages related to your podcast

Podcast advertising is currently in the early adopter stage, but one option to consider is Podtrac (**www.podtrac.com**). Podtrac creates a free audience survey and custom media kit for participating podcasters who are then eligible to participate in their advertising auction.

If podcast advertising is something you're interested in pursuing, you should wait until you have a reasonable number of subscribers before seeking advertisers. No one wants to advertise on a podcast with just a few subscribers. Focus on developing an audience, and then sign up for an advertising program.

Web-Savvy in Action

Elmer is the author of a series of books on home-based business who produces a popular podcast in a talk show format. In each podcast, he covers an area of interest to home-based business owners and interviews an expert in that field. In addition to providing useful information for his audience, these guests usually promote their appearance on his podcast on their own sites and blogs. To give his podcast a professional touch, Elmer adds an introduction using podsafe music.

Elmer hopes his podcast generates revenue as well as promotes his books. On his website and blog, he provides detailed information on his consulting services and seminars and recommends affiliate products that his audience may be interested in buying. At appropriate times throughout his podcasts, Elmer discusses these products and services and mentions his website URL.

▶ See chapter 9, "Promoting Your Book with Online Advertising," Generating Advertising Revenue

Promoting Your Podcast

To develop an audience for your podcast, you need to let people know it's available.

Promoting Your Podcast on Your Website and Blog

Once you create a podcast, the first thing you should do is to let your blog and website visitors know about it. One of the easiest ways to do this is to add feed subscription buttons, also called chicklets, enabling your readers to subscribe to your podcast feed.

To add these buttons, you need to generate HTML code that includes information about your feed and insert this code into your web page or blog. Don't worry. Generating the HTML code is usually an automated process. There are several ways to do this:

- If you use FeedBurner, click the Publicize tab and then the Chicklet Chooser button to generate the HTML code for the buttons you want to use, including those for podcast readers such as Odeo, PodNova, My Yahoo!, and more.
- Use the HTML code your podcast hosting service provides you.
- Go to the websites of the podcast readers whose buttons you want to add to your page to find instructions on how to add their feed subscription buttons.
- If you use TypePad, the ability to add a podcast link to your sidebar is built into the existing template.
- If you use WordPress, consider PodPress (**www.podpress.org**).

Tip If you're planning to issue an online press release, consider PRWeb's press release podcasting service (**www.prweb. com**). For an added fee, PRWeb records a podcast interview with you and posts it with your release.

▸ See chapter 11, "Promoting Your Book with Online Press Releases," Distributing Your Online Press Release

Pinging Update Services

When you complete a new podcast, use a ping utility to notify multiple update services that you have a new show. Using a utility to notify multiple services with a single entry is a big timesaver. For example, you could notify Fresh Podcasts, Odeo, PodNova, iPodder, Podscope, BlogDigger, and Audio.weblogs.com all on one form. Some free ping utilities to consider include AllPodcasts.com (**www.allpodcasts.com**) and King Ping (**www.kping.com**).

Submitting Your Podcast to Podcast Directories

Listing your podcast in the most popular podcast directories also helps new listeners discover your podcast. Here are some good choices to start:

- iTunes (**www.apple.com/itunes/podcasts**)
- Odeo (**www.odeo.com**)
- Podcast Alley (**www.podcastalley.com**)
- PodNova (**www.podnova.com**)
- Yahoo! Podcasts (**podcasts.yahoo.com**)

If you want to find more places to submit your podcast, search on your favorite search engine for "podcast directory."

Web-Savvy in Action

Molly is the author of a memoir about raising a family of ten children. To promote her book, Molly creates a "slice of life" podcast filled with humorous stories about her family. The main challenge for Molly is that her target audience generally isn't very familiar with podcasting. She features her podcast on her website home page and provides a link to her podcast feed. Few of her readers subscribe, however, and many people at her in-person presentations admit that they didn't understand podcasting.

To educate her audience about podcasting, and increase her number of listeners, Molly reworks the content on her website to provide more basic background information, referring to her podcast as an "Internet radio show." By providing direct links to listen online, her audience begins to develop. As her listeners become more comfortable with the concept of podcasting, they refer to Molly's advanced information about feeds, subscribing via a podcast reader, and playing podcasts on iPods and other MP3 players.

Podcasting Step-by-Step

Podcasting helps you connect with—and entertain—your audience using the spoken word. Having your own "online radio show" is now easier than ever. Here's your step-by-step "to do" list:

- ☐ Research podcasting and verify that you understand the basic concepts
- ☐ Listen and subscribe to several podcasts to get a first-hand view of how podcasting technologies work
- ☐ Create a concept and theme for your podcast and plan several shows
- ☐ Research and choose your podcasting tools and hosting technologies (don't go overboard on expensive equipment when you're first starting out with podcasting)
- ☐ Record your podcast, either on your computer using recording software and a microphone or by phone
- ☐ Save your podcast as an MP3 file and upload it to your server (many podcast hosting services simplify this step)
- ☐ Create a podcast feed with FeedBurner or another tool
- ☐ Publish your podcast
- ☐ Promote your podcast on your website, blog, and ezine; on the web; and in search engines and blog directories
- ☐ Consider incorporating advertising into your podcast when your subscriber volume warrants it

6

Promoting Your Book with an Ezine

An ezine, short for electronic magazine, is an online newsletter sent via email. An ezine is another effective way of communicating with your target audience. You can quickly and inexpensively set up a basic ezine and start sending it regularly to subscribers. By posting past issues on your site, you can reach an even wider audience.

Quick Fact	Targeted email marketing campaigns can generate nine times more revenue and eighteen times more profit than broadcast mailings. —*Source: JupiterResearch*

Planning Your Ezine

As with everything else you do to market your book, creating a successful ezine requires careful planning.

Checking Out the Competition

Before creating your own ezine, check out your competitors. You may already subscribe to several industry ezines, but now's the time to sign up for others, looking at the process from a new perspective. In addition to the ezines published by your direct competitors, also sign up for those in your general industry and by authors who write in other genres. This gives you a wider variety of ezines to analyze.

If you're worried about potential spam, use a free email account, such as one from Yahoo! Mail, Gmail, or Hotmail instead of using your personal email address. You can always unsubscribe to these ezines later if the volume gets too overwhelming.

As you sign up for ezines and start to read them, ask yourself these questions:

- What email marketing service does the ezine use to send emails? What is your impression of this service?
- How easy is it to subscribe?
- Where is the sign-up form on the website?
- Is the ezine aesthetically pleasing? Is it well designed?
- Does the ezine offer both text and HTML options?
- Is the content of true value? Or is it an obvious sales pitch?

After receiving a number of competitor ezines for several weeks, you'll get a good feel for what is currently available, what appeals to you, and how to position your own ezine strategically into the mix.

Tip   Complete the subscription form on my website (**www. websavvywriter.com**) to sign up for my ezine, The Web-Savvy Writer.

Establishing Goals for Your Ezine

Your ezine should have a goal, or in some cases, multiple goals. The first goal of any ezine should be to provide quality information that your audience can't easily find elsewhere. Without this, you won't be able to retain subscribers and the marketing potential of your ezine will be lost. After that, focus on goals specific to your promotional efforts. For example, you may want to:

- Increase book sales
- Generate revenue from the sale of additional products and services
- Promote yourself as a consultant and speaker

Selecting an Email Marketing Service

Choosing an email marketing service is one of the most important decisions you need to make as you plan your ezine, second only to content considerations. An email marketing service automates many of the tasks required to publish an ezine including subscription management and ezine delivery. Most services also provide templates that you can use to create your ezine quickly and easily, including both text and HTML formats. Another feature to look for is the ability to generate analytical reports about your ezine delivery and response rates. You want to know who is opening your email, who isn't getting your ezine, who is clicking on your ezine links, and much more. Some services to consider include:

- Aweber (**www.aweber.com**)
- Constant Contact (**www.constantcontact.com**)
- iContact (**www.icontact.com**)

If you want to combine email marketing with ecommerce functionality, consider the following full-featured shopping cart solutions:

- 1ShoppingCart (**www.1shoppingcart.com**)
- Professional Cart Solutions (**www.profcs.com**)

Here are some questions to ask that will help you select the right email marketing service for your needs:

- Does the service offer ezine templates?
- Can you sign up for a free "test drive" to see how well you like the service?
- Do you want to use autoresponders? If so, does the service provide this feature?
- How much does the service cost? Is there staggered pricing based on volume? Be sure to consider where you want to be in six months when making decisions based on pricing. Changing services can be time-consuming.
- Does the service provide reports so you can analyze your results?
- If you're anticipating a high volume of direct sales from your site, have you considered a full-service ecommerce solution that includes email marketing?

Tip An alternative to using an email marketing service is to use email software to manage and distribute your ezine, such as phplist (**www.phplist.com**) or MailList King (**www.xequte.com/maillistking/index.html**). The advantages of the do-it-yourself approach are that you can maintain control of the mailing list data and avoid paying monthly fees. On the downside, this option requires more technical skill and can be more complex and time-consuming.

▶ See chapter 7, "Selling and Promoting Your Book with Ecommerce," Full-Service Shopping Cart Solutions

Taking Spam Seriously

Unsolicited email known as spam is a serious issue to email marketers. Don't let fear of spam prevent you from establishing a successful email marketing campaign, but do educate yourself on spam legislation to ensure your ezine complies. Here are some tips to help you avoid any problems with spam:

- Require that subscribers sign up for your ezine. Don't just start sending your new publication to everyone you know, or worse, to people you don't know. This is known as opt-in, permission-based marketing.
- Post a privacy policy on your site and stick to it.

- Enable your ezine subscribers to easily unsubscribe, or opt out, of your ezine by including instructions. Remove each subscriber who opts out immediately.
- Include contact information in every ezine issue. If you don't want to use your home address, rent a mailbox.
- Be wary of buying lists of subscribers for your ezine. Although reputable list brokers do exist, many harvest names from the web without permission. In general, it's best to grow your own subscriber list by allowing people to opt in to your ezine.
- Keep up with the latest spam legislation and trends. Some sites to review include the eMarketing Association (**www. emarketingassociation.com/spam.htm**) and Spam Laws (**www.spamlaws.com**).

Fortunately, email marketing services are very aware of the seriousness of spam. Most provide tools to help you comply with the legal requirements surrounding email marketing.

Avoiding Anti-Spam Filters

An anti-spam filter is a tool that helps distinguish between your real mail and junk mail spam, usually placing email deemed spam in a folder separate from your regular email. This is great if you're the email recipient. It's not so great if you're sending legitimate opt-in email to your list and it's flagged by an anti-spam filter.

To avoid these filters, be aware of the words that trigger them. Some words that frequently attract the attention of a spam filter include:

- Buy
- Free
- Money
- Order
- Sale

Although you can try to trick the system by using creative spelling such as "fr*ee" instead of "free," it's best to create real content that avoids the filter. You can always link to a page on your website that provides detailed sales information for the products you want to sell.

To check your email for possible problems before you send it, try the Lyris ContentChecker (**www.lyris.com/resources/contentchecker**).

Ten Content Ideas for Your Ezine

The content you include in your ezine can make the difference between success and failure. Even though your goal may be to sell books, services, or other products, your ezine must offer value to your subscribers or else they won't continue to subscribe. Here are ten ideas to get you started:

From the Editor

A personal message from you, the ezine author, is a must for any successful ezine. To achieve your goals, you need to connect with your audience. Getting to know you is an important part of developing that connection. In this section, you can offer your thoughts about industry events, describe what's happening in your own life, preface the content of this issue of your ezine, or offer motivational advice. A photo can also help personalize this section of your ezine. Be wary about starting with an overt sales message. At this stage, you want to connect, not sell.

Feature Article

The feature article is the foundation of your ezine. Select it with care. You want to create the type of article that makes your subscribers look forward to each issue, knowing that they will learn something of value. By crafting useful articles that directly relate to your current promotional efforts, you provide a valuable service to your subscribers as well as potentially increase the number of people interested in purchasing what you have to offer.

One of the advantages of creating good feature articles for your ezine is that you can recycle this content for added publicity. After you publish your feature, post it to your own website, reprint it on other sites, post it to free article sites, or rework the content to include in a blog, podcast, or other form of communication.

Guest Features

Many ezines include guest articles by other non-competing authors. Why would you want to include another writer's work in *your* ezine? Well, there are several reasons. You can:

- Beef up the content in your ezine without any additional work on your part
- Add more value to your ezine subscribers by providing additional information on related topics
- Elevate the prestige of a new ezine by including a guest feature written by a well-known figure in your industry
- Increase your subscribers by trading feature articles with another ezine publisher (your article appears in that publisher's ezine as well, introducing you to potential new subscribers)
- Generate affiliate income by promoting the products of your guest authors

Subscriber Tips

Publishing tips from your subscribers can provide unique content for your ezine as well as involve subscribers in your publication.

Editorials about Recent Trends in Your Industry

If you're an expert in your field, your subscribers want to know your opinions about what's going on in your industry. This is your opportunity to demonstrate your expertise and present your platform.

Industry News

In addition to providing editorial comment, you can simply report on the latest news in your industry or niche. If your subscribers know they will stay current on the latest news with your ezine, they will be more likely to open and read each issue.

Tip	Another spin on this idea is to include news about yourself, including your latest books, appearances, courses, seminars, and more. Publish self-serving news judiciously, however. Subscribers do want to know what's new with you, but your ezine can't come across solely as an advertisement for your books and services. You'll risk losing subscribers otherwise.

Links to Excerpts from Your Books

Offering ezine subscribers some selected content from your book, which isn't available elsewhere, can be viewed as a "gift" and helps promote sales.

▶ See chapter 1, "Promoting Your Book with a Website," Book Excerpts

Interviews

Linking to a text transcript or downloadable audio of an interview you've recently given provides worthwhile information to your audience as well as further demonstrates your standing as an expert in your field. Another option is to include the actual text of the interview in your ezine, with permission from the original publication, of course. A third idea is for you to interview experts in complementary fields. These experts would probably be happy to publicize this interview, and your ezine, on their own sites.

Quizzes

Quizzes are a popular item in many publications. Create educational and interesting quizzes about your area of expertise and include them in your ezine or on your website.

Coupons

Another way to promote your books and services without cluttering your feature content with sales hype is to publish special subscriber-only coupons at the end of your ezine. Not only does this highlight what you have to offer, but it also emphasizes the benefits of subscribing to your ezine. Some examples include:

- Discounts off the price of your books, services, courses, consulting, and more
- Two-for-one specials
- Free offer with purchase

Several email marketing services, such as Constant Contact, have an automated coupon feature that makes it easy to offer discount coupons to your subscribers.

Creating Your Ezine

With a plan in place, it's time to start designing your ezine. Although it's a lot of up-front work, the time spent on producing a regular ezine decreases after you establish a solid format and system.

Creating an Ezine Template

Because many email services provide ready-made ezine templates, you should wait until you've selected a service before finalizing your design. You can use a template as is, customize an existing template, or create your own from scratch. In general, your ezine should have the same color scheme and similar design to your website and other marketing collateral.

In addition to choosing colors, styles, and fonts, you need to establish the structure of your ezine before finalizing its template. The content suggestions in the previous section should give you some good ideas for your own ezine. A sample ezine structure could look something like this:

- From the Editor
- Promotional Announcement
- Feature Article
- In the News

- Guest Article
- Reader Tips
- Advertising
- Coupon

Tip   There is an ongoing debate on which format is better, a text ezine or an HTML ezine (with graphics and formatting similar to a web page). Most email marketing services enable you to deliver both text and HTML ezines, so I recommend that you offer subscribers a choice of format.

Setting a Schedule

You also need to set a schedule for your ezine. Weekly, biweekly, and monthly are the most common options. More than once a week could drive away subscribers. Less than monthly could make them forget about you.

Tip   If you're concerned about the time it takes to create an ezine, you can start with a monthly format and then consider a more frequent schedule if it starts to generate results. Alternatively, you could hire a virtual assistant or other service to help you with the details of your ezine creation and distribution.

Performing a Test Run

Most email marketing services enable you to do a test run of your ezine delivery before going live. Your test run should include delivery in both HTML and text formats as well as to several common email providers such as Gmail, Hotmail, and Yahoo! Mail.

If you don't have accounts with all of these providers, create free accounts for testing purposes. Also, find friends and colleagues who have email accounts with popular ISPs and ask them for input on the delivery and appearance of your ezine. It's better to find potential glitches at this stage than when you actually start publishing.

Profiting from Your Ezine

Obviously, you want to profit from your ezine by selling more of your books, products, and services. You can also generate ezine profits by accepting ezine advertising. One way to attract advertisers is simply to indicate in your ezine that you accept advertising and direct potential advertisers to more information on your website.

Also, consider exchanging ads with other ezines targeting the same audience. You won't actually earn any income this way, but you can potentially increase your subscriber base.

Quick Fact	Email marketing spending will grow to $1.1 billion by 2010, and the volume of spam messages per consumer will decrease by 13 percent a year during this same period. —*Source: JupiterResearch*

▶ See chapter 9, "Promoting Your Book with Online Advertising"

Web-Savvy in Action	Brianna, Lauren, and Kate are romance novelists who all live in the same metropolitan area. Between the three of them, they have 35 novels in print, all targeting the same audience. Brianna suggests to Lauren and Kate that they join forces and create a joint monthly ezine that promotes the works of all three authors. Although they use the same format each month, they rotate content creation responsibilities with each taking the lead every third month. The group ezine offers many advantages to the three novelists. They're able to connect with their audience on a monthly basis, yet the work involved in creating the ezine is far less than an individual ezine. In addition, by cross promoting their work, they're able to find new readers who many not otherwise have discovered their books.

Eight Ways to Promote Your Ezine

Even a well-written, well-targeted ezine won't succeed without enough people reading it. You need subscribers, but not just any subscribers. You need to attract the type of subscriber who is genuinely interested in your subject matter. Try these eight ideas for increasing your subscriber base.

Website Subscription Form

Place an ezine subscription form on every page of your website, such as in your site header or navigation sidebar that repeats on every page. If you have a blog, also include an ezine sign-up box on one of your sidebars. Ensuring subscriber privacy helps you increase the number of sign-ups.

Subscription Incentives

To encourage new ezine subscribers, offer something of value in exchange for signing up. This item should be easy to deliver, such as a special report or ecourse, and directly relate to your ezine and book subject matter.

For example, to increase the number of subscribers to my ezine, *The Web-Savvy Writer*, I offer a free copy of a special report. Subscribers receive access to a download page when they sign up for the ezine, so I don't have to do anything manually and the subscribers immediately get their "freebie."

Website Promotional Page for Your Ezine

Even if you have an ezine subscription form on every page of your website, you still should create a special page that details your ezine's benefits. In addition to providing more information about all the great things your ezine has to offer, describe any free bonuses subscribers receive when they sign up. An added advantage is that if you properly optimize this page, search engines direct traffic from people searching for an ezine on your topic.

Website Ezine Archive

Although some ezine publishers worry that people won't subscribe to their ezine if they archive back issues on their sites, the advantages of doing this usually outweigh the disadvantages. Archiving increases the amount of keyword searchable pages on your site and, as a result, increases the number of people who find your site through search engines.

Recycled Ezine Content

If you did your homework, you've already signed up for numerous competing ezines. If any of these ezines publishes guest authors and is a good match for the audience you want to target, consider submitting your articles to that publisher for possible inclusion as a guest feature. Also, look for related websites that publish guest articles and submit there as well.

Article Marketing

Another option is posting your published ezine articles on article marketing sites that distribute free articles to other sites and ezines.

▶ See chapter 12, "Promoting Your Book with Article Marketing"

Viral Marketing

Encourage your subscribers to forward your ezine to their friends and associates by suggesting this in every ezine issue. In your subscription section, remind subscribers who were forwarded your ezine to subscribe on their own. Offering a "reward" for subscribing, normally the same incentive you offer on your website, can increase subscriptions.

Ezine Directories

Although promoting your ezine directly to your target audience generates the majority of your subscribers, it's still a good idea to list your ezine in directories. Some to try include:

- BestEzines (**www.bestezines.com**)
- EzineHub (**www.ezinehub.com**)

- Jogena's (**www.jogena.com**)
- New-List.com (**www.new-list.com**)

To locate additional ezine directories, do a search on your favorite search engine for "ezine directory." You'll find hundreds of choices. Some should be a good match for your ezine.

If you want to list your ezine in as many directories as possible, consider automating the task with ezine submission software such as Ezine Announcer (**www.ezineannouncer.com**). Using ezine submission software, you can submit automatically to multiple ezine directories and lists as well as track your progress. Quantity, however, doesn't always equal quality. You want members of your target audience to sign up for your ezine, not just anyone online. In general, the wider your prospective audience, the more useful automation is. If you publish an ezine directed to a tightly targeted market, you're probably better off focusing your efforts directly on that market.

Web-Savvy in Action

Phyllis is a registered dietician and author of a book on food allergies who publishes an ezine on this topic. Each issue includes a feature article with meaningful tips related to food allergies. She also provides guest articles by experts on healthy living including several from a well-known allergist. Her "Readers' Write" section encourages subscribers to submit questions related to food allergies, which she regularly answers. Her subscribers look forward to each issue and many save, print, or forward issues due to the important information they provide.

At the end of each ezine, Phyllis offers a coupon for discounts on several special reports she publishes and on her consulting services. She also provides a link to purchase her book on Amazon.com. When her subscribers are ready to buy, they think of Phyllis first because of the valuable information she offers them throughout the year.

Ezine Publishing Step-by-Step

Publishing an ezine helps you develop an ongoing connection with your audience in exchange for providing relevant content for them on a regular basis. Here's your step-by-step "to do" list:

- ☐ Research ezine publishing and verify that you understand the basic concepts
- ☐ Subscribe to several competitive ezines to get an idea of what works and what doesn't work
- ☐ Plan a content strategy and schedule for your ezine
- ☐ Select and sign up with an email marketing service
- ☐ Design your ezine template
- ☐ Create your first issue
- ☐ Perform a test run to ensure a smooth delivery
- ☐ Create a subscription form for your ezine and include it on your website and blog
- ☐ Develop and execute a promotion plan for your ezine
- ☐ Analyze your statistics and revise your content and delivery strategies if needed

7

Selling and Promoting Your Book
with Ecommerce

Being able to sell books, products, and services online is a goal of many authors. Whether you develop a complex ecommerce system or simply generate affiliate revenue from the sale of your books, there are ample opportunities for selling your work online. An added bonus is that your sales efforts can also result in additional publicity.

Quick Fact	As of January 2008, more than 875 million people worldwide have shopped online. More than 41 percent of these shoppers purchased books online in the last three months. —*Source: ACNielsen*

Determining What You Can—and Can't—Sell Online

Depending on whether you self-published or published through a traditional publisher, there could be limits on what you can independently sell online.

Ecommerce for Traditionally Published Authors

If you published your book through a traditional publisher, your publisher will take care of making it available for sale on ecommerce sites such as Amazon.com and Barnes & Noble through their normal distribution channels. In general, books are listed in online bookstores through a distributor such as Ingram or Baker & Taylor.

Tip	The best-known ecommerce site for books is Amazon.com, which enables independent publishers to list books through regular distribution channels as well as through its Advantage program. Because there are so many opportunities for selling and marketing your books on Amazon, I've devoted an entire chapter (chapter 8) to this topic.

To sell traditionally published books on your website, look into affiliate programs such as the Amazon Associates program (**www.amazon.com/associates**) or the Barnes & Noble Affiliate program (**www.barnesandnoble.com/affiliate**). With these programs, you can promote your book on your site and provide a link to your book's page on the online bookstore's site. When someone makes a purchase, you receive a commission on the sale.

▶ See chapter 8, "Selling and Promoting Your Book on Amazon.com," Making Money with Amazon Associates

Another option is to sell autographed copies of your books directly from your website. Readers enjoy autographed books even if you're not a famous author … yet. You can often purchase copies of your book at a discount from your publisher, which makes this a win-win opportunity for both you and your readers.

Tip	The rest of this chapter focuses on selling your books and related products on the web. If you published your book through a traditional publisher and don't have additional products to sell, you can continue to the next chapter.

Ecommerce for Self-Publishers

If you self-published your book and own your ISBN, you're free to pursue any ecommerce opportunities you choose in addition to the distribution you already have. Most book distribution services take care of listing your book on major sites such as Amazon, Barnes & Noble, and so forth. Your goal should be to find other avenues to sell your book online. Just be sure that any distribution channels you use aren't restrictive and prohibit you from other options.

Tip	An ISBN (International Standard Book Number) is a 13-digit number that serves as a unique identifier for an individual book, including ebooks. Unless the author is also the publisher, the ISBN is assigned to the publisher of the book, not the author.
	If you're self-publishing and want to own your own ISBN, be sure to verify this with the company you use to produce and print your books. Several subsidy publishers provide ISBNs for you, but your books are registered with their name as the publisher, not yours. To register an ISBN, go to the ISBN website (**www.isbn.org**).

One of the easiest ways for self-published authors to make more money is to sell ebook versions of their print books. In addition to selling ebooks directly on your site, covered later in this chapter, you can make your ebook available for sale on other websites. Some good options include:

- **Lulu** (**www.lulu.com**). Earn 75 percent commission on all ebooks for sale on the Lulu Marketplace. Lulu also enables you to optimize your ebook for use on an iPhone or the Sony Reader Digital Book.

- **Booklocker** (www.booklocker.com). Lists your nonfiction ebook at no charge if it's already formatted as a PDF. Pays a 70 percent commission on sales.
- **Mobipocket eBookBase** (www.mobipocket.com/ebookbase). Distributes Mobipocket ebooks through a network of ebooksellers such as Mobipocket.com, Fictionwise.com, CyberRead, and many more. There is no charge to join the network and you receive a 50 percent commission on books sold.
- **eBookMall** (www.ebookmall.com). Pays 50 percent commission on ebook sales. Charges a small listing fee per title. Conversion to Adobe Reader, Microsoft Reader, and Mobipocket formats available for an additional fee.

Tip	Formatting your content for viewing on the Amazon Kindle wireless reading device is another option, particularly if you're interested in selling your content on Amazon.

▸ See chapter 8, "Selling and Promoting Your Book on Amazon.com," Amazon Kindle

Ecommerce Opportunities for Supplemental Products

The ecommerce suggestions in this chapter also work well for selling original content that supplements your print books—both traditionally published and self-published—such as ebooks, special reports, online courses, teleseminars, audio CDs, DVDs, and other information products. Or, you could develop your own line of products related to your books content, such as a cookbook author selling cookware, an author of a craft book selling original crafts, and so forth.

Web-Savvy in Action	Valentina is a nature photographer who is the author of a photography book on national parks of the American West. She would like to sell calendars, posters, and greeting cards that display her nature images as a way to supplement her income and promote both her book and her growing photography business. Valentina doesn't want to invest a large amount of money on this new venture and decides to try out her concept at no cost with a CafePress (**www.cafepress.com**) basic store, which she promotes on her website and with search engine optimization techniques.

▸ See chapter 15, "Twelve More Ways to Promote Your Book Online," Supplemental Information Products

Selling Books from Your Website

If you want to sell your books directly from your website, you need ecommerce functionality. Selling books on your site can be a good source of income even if your book is available on big sites such as Amazon and Barnes & Noble. You can usually purchase copies of your book in bulk from your printer at discount prices, which makes direct sales even more profitable for you. Autographing the books you sell from your site increases their value in the eyes of many readers. Selling an ebook version of your print book is another good idea, as discussed in the previous section.

Evaluating Ecommerce Solutions

Before getting started, however, consider your options. The first decision is narrowing down the type of solution you're looking for. You can implement a robust, full-service ecommerce solution or simply sign up with a service that enables you to accept credit card payments. If you want to sell digital downloads such as ebooks, you'll need to integrate an additional solution with a basic online payment processing service like PayPal or Google Checkout.

Choosing the appropriate ecommerce solution for your needs depends on your answer to several questions:

- Are you selling print books, ebooks, or both?
- What sales volume do you anticipate? This is often hard to predict, but you need some idea of how much you think you'll sell per month to choose the right solution.
- Do you require additional services such as autoresponders, ezine delivery, sales analytics, or affiliate programs?
- Do you want to sell products and services other than your books? There's a long list of items you may want to sell: special reports, audio CDs, DVDs, teleseminars, consulting and coaching services, software, music, digital art, calendars, forms, as well as other products related to your book's content.
- How much technical skill do you have? Some shopping cart solutions are very simple to implement; others require more advanced technical skills. If you don't have these skills yourself, you could have to hire someone to help you get a more complex ecommerce solution up and running.

When you have the answers to these important questions, compare several solutions to find the one that meets all your requirements at the best possible price. Be sure to analyze the total cost of each solution. Calculate all costs, including setup fees, monthly fees, and commissions. To factor in the cost of commissions, estimate your monthly sales volume and use the same sales estimates in all your comparisons.

Basic Online Payment Solutions

If you're new to ecommerce and just want something simple to sell books from your website, consider PayPal or Google Checkout.

PayPal

PayPal (**www.paypal.com**) is a popular online payment service that's particularly suitable for authors who are new to ecommerce and want something easy to use or anticipate a modest sales volume.

PayPal charges no setup, monthly, or gateway merchant fees and enables you to accept payment by credit card (Visa, MasterCard, American Express, and Discover), bank transfer, or PayPal account. For each sale, you pay a variable commission plus a small transaction fee. PayPal also offers an easy-to-use shopping cart.

Ecommerce options to consider include:

- **Website Payments Standard**. With this plan, customers shop on your website and pay on PayPal via a page that you customize. Website Payments Standard requires only basic HTML skills to implement (that is, you copy the generated HTML code and place it on your web page).
- **Website Payments Pro**. This plan enables your customers to both shop and pay on your website, an advantage if you want to provide an integrated ecommerce experience for them. To use this plan, you need skills in implementing web services and APIs or the willingness to hire someone with these skills to set up the ecommerce system on your site.
- **Email Payments**. Email Payments is suited to authors who sell consulting and coaching services instead of physical or digital products and want a way to bill their customers by email. This plan requires limited technical skills.

Google Checkout

Google offers its own online payment solution called Google Checkout (**checkout.google.com**).

With Google Checkout, you pay a commission plus a small transaction fee for each sale. Google Checkout charges no setup, monthly, or gateway merchant fees and enables you to accept payment by credit card. If you use Google AdWords to advertise your products, you can add a Google Checkout badge to your ads to encourage further sales.

There are several ways to use Google Checkout. You can integrate it with your existing shopping cart (including integration with custom-built carts via an API), sign up for a Google-supporting shopping cart, sell individual items easily with Buy Now buttons, or send email invoices.

Digital Downloads Solutions

If you want to sell digital downloads such as ebooks, you need to choose a solution that handles the automated delivery of such files and integrates with the online payment service you choose, such as PayPal or Google Checkout.

Here are three good options for selling digital downloads from your website:

- **PayLoadz** (**www.payloadz.com**). PayLoadz uses PayPal or Google Checkout online payment processing, but it offers additional features including automated delivery of digital downloads, a built-in affiliate system enabling others to help you sell your products, and support for selling your products on auction sites like eBay. PayLoadz offers two pricing structures: a flat monthly fee based on sales revenue or a percentage of total sales. If your sales volume is less than $100 per month, there is no monthly fee.

- **E-Junkie** (**www.e-junkie.com**). E-Junkie offers automated delivery of digital downloads, integration with PayPal and Google Checkout, built-in support for Google Analytics, an affiliate program you can use with both digital and physical products as well as integration with SwiftCD (**www.swiftcd.com**) for CD and DVD fulfillment. Pricing begins at $5 per month for up to 10 products with no transaction fees.

- **ClickBank** (**www.clickbank.com**). With ClickBank, you can accept payment via a variety of credit card options as well as PayPal. One of ClickBank's most popular features is its affiliate program, which it heavily promotes to webmasters looking for affiliate products to sell. ClickBank charges a modest setup fee, but there are no monthly fees. You just pay a small transaction fee plus a percentage of your sales price. If you participate in the affiliate program, your fees are greatly reduced.

Web-Savvy in Action	Cody is the author of a California adventure guidebook published by a leading travel publisher. As an avid hiker, he would like to sell a series of short illustrated hiking guides as downloadable PDFs from his website.
	Because Cody isn't sure of his sales volume and doesn't plan to sell any other products or services, he decides to start with a low-cost ecommerce solution that emphasizes digital downloads.

Full-Service Shopping Cart Solutions

A full-service shopping cart enables you to integrate ecommerce into your website and combine this functionality with other online marketing features you may want, including:

- Autoresponders, which enable you to send automated emails
- Recurring billing, useful for membership sites or subscriptions

- Ad tracking and coupons
- Affiliate programs, which enable others to sell your products for a commission
- Email distribution, including ezines
- The ability to sell digital downloads, services, and online courses in addition to physical products

Shopping cart solutions with extensive features are a good choice for authors who sell multiple types of products and want to integrate features such as autoresponders, affiliate marketing, and ezines into one package. A good full-service solution to consider is 1ShoppingCart.com (**www.1shoppingcart.com**).

Because of monthly service and merchant account fees, you should feel confident in your anticipated sales volume before selecting this option. If you anticipate a low sales volume or just want to try out ecommerce with a few items, then look at lower cost options like PayPal or Google Checkout.

Web-Savvy in Action	Ralf is the author of a book on real estate investing published by a leading traditional publisher. He has also created several special reports and audio CDs on this topic that he wants to market to his readers. The reports and CDs are available as both physical products and digital downloads. To promote his offerings, Ralf plans to publish a weekly ezine, provide a free ecourse via autoresponder, and offer affiliate commissions to people who help sell his products. Thanks to these efforts, he anticipates a reasonably high sales volume. Ralf would like to streamline his operations as much as possible and not deal with multiple service providers. Based on his requirements and projected sales revenue, Ralf chooses a shopping cart solution that includes ecommerce functionality, digital download capability, ezine distribution, autoresponders, and affiliate integration.

Selling Books on eBay

Another option to consider is selling your books on the online auction site eBay (**www.ebay.com**). Although this option isn't suitable for all authors, it can work well for certain types of books and supplemental products. Options include having customers bid on your book, making your books available at a fixed Buy It Now price, or selling digital download ebooks.

Quick Fact	In May 2008, eBay received 66.2 million unique visitors in the U.S. alone. —*Source: Nielsen//NetRating*

Selling Books on Online Shopping Sites

Another idea for selling your books online is to get listed on online shopping sites. Sites that serve your niche are often the best, but general shopping sites offer exposure as well. Here are three to consider:

- **Froogle (froogle.google.com).** Froogle is Google's shopping search engine. It's s a great bargain, too—it's free. You simply upload information about your products, which appear in Froogle search results when someone is looking for what you have to sell.
- **Live Product Search (search.live.com/productupload).** Microsoft will list your products free in its Live Product Search index (**www.live.com**).
- **Shopzilla (www.shopzilla.com).** There's no cost to get listed in Shopzilla, a cost-per-click online shopping search engine; you pay only when someone clicks through to your site. Shopzilla listings also appear on BizRate and AOL's InStore.com.

Ecommerce Step-by-Step

Many authors find that selling their own products online is highly profitable. Even if you publish with a traditional publisher, you can profit from creating products that complement your books. Here's your step-by-step "to do" list:

☐ Determine what products you want to sell online (print books, ebooks, audio downloads, CDs, special reports, and so forth)

☐ Research and select an ecommerce solution, such as a full-service shopping cart or online payment service, that's appropriate for your product mix and sales volume

☐ Implement the ecommerce solution to start selling from your website

☐ Research and implement sales opportunities on auction sites such as eBay and other online shopping sites

8

Selling and Promoting Your Book
on Amazon.com

Amazon.com (**www.amazon.com**) is one of the best-known online bookstores in the world. With a worldwide audience of millions of customers, you want your book available for purchase on Amazon. The good news is that it's easy to list your book on Amazon, and just as easy to create an inviting book detail page for prospective customers to view.

Quick Fact	In August 2008, Amazon received 57.9 million unique visitors in the U.S. alone. *— Source: Nielsen//NetRatings*

The information covered in this chapter focuses on Amazon's U.S. site, but much of it also applies to Amazon's sites for other countries including Canada, the U.K., France, Germany, Austria, Japan, and China.

Selling Your Books on Amazon

If you published your book with a traditional publisher, your publisher will take care of getting your book into the Amazon catalog through its distribution channels. Even though most of the work will be done for you, you should still work with your publisher to create the best possible detail page for your book. Also consider joining AmazonConnect, discussed later in this chapter.

Tip	Amazon offers a detailed online guide (**www.amazon.com/publishers**), which covers the options available for publishers and authors.

Self-publishers have several choices if your book isn't already available on Amazon through your own distribution channels. These include Amazon's on-demand publishing services, Amazon Advantage, and Amazon Kindle.

Amazon On-Demand Publishing

Amazon's on-demand publishing services provide a way to produce products as well as sell them. Through its subsidiary BookSurge (**www.booksurge.com**), Amazon offers on-demand book publishing and distribution. Its subsidiary CreateSpace (**www.createspace.com**) enables you to publish on-demand print and audio books, CDs, and DVDs. Pricing and distribution options differ with BookSurge and CreateSpace so be sure to compare their current programs if you feel one of these solutions may be right for you. In particular, if owning your own ISBN is important to you (so that your company is listed as the publisher and not the company printing your book), verify this with any publishing service you're considering.

Self-publishers can also use other on-demand publishing services to create books, CDs, and DVDs to sell on Amazon. If you prefer to use a service other than BookSurge or CreateSpace, determine what your book's availability on Amazon would be. There is quite a bit of controversy surrounding the availability of on-demand titles in Amazon's catalog, so it pays to analyze the current situation before making a decision.

Web-Savvy in Action

Violet is the author of a book on knitting who wants to supplement her book royalties by creating an instructional knitting DVD. She creates her DVD with the help of a small local studio, but she has a limited budget for duplication, distribution, and marketing.

She decides to try a test marketing campaign using CreateSpace, Amazon's on-demand DVD publishing service. Violet lists her DVD in the Amazon catalog and produces only the number of DVDs sold. If sales increase, she plans to consider higher volume DVD duplication. If not, she can continue to sell small quantities with little investment.

Amazon Advantage

If you choose not to use either of Amazon's on-demand publishing services and your book isn't available in the Amazon catalog, consider signing up for Amazon Advantage (**www.amazon.com/advantage**).

You need to hold the North American distribution rights to your book to sign up for the Advantage program. Advantage charges a small annual fee plus a commission of 55 percent for each book sold. The benefits of joining Advantage include 24-hour shipping availability for your books, fulfillment services (including customer service, credit card processing, and shipping), automatic reorder notifications, and monthly payments.

Tip

Advantage isn't only for authors whose books aren't already available in the Amazon catalog. If you're a self-publisher and your book doesn't ship within 24 hours, you may want to join Advantage to gain access to 24-hour shipping among other features.

Amazon Kindle

Formatting your content for viewing on the Amazon Kindle wireless reading device is another publishing option. You receive 35 percent of the suggested retail price that you set for each title. The Amazon Kindle site (**dtp.amazon.com**) offers detailed directions on how to format your content for Kindle.

Creating Your Book's Detail Page

Once your book is on Amazon, you need to capture the attention of potential customers. Creating a quality book detail page loaded with intriguing content is the first step.

Descriptive Content for Your Book's Detail Page

In order to pique the interest of potential readers, your book's detail page should be rich with content. In addition to basic information about your book such as title, author, and publication date, you can also include the following:

- A book description
- An excerpt
- Table of contents
- Reviews
- Cover art

- Author bio
- Author comments
- Back cover and inside flap copy
- Additional images
- Reading group guide content

Most text fields are limited to 1,000 words, but this still provides plenty of opportunity for enough quality information to motivate prospects to buy. If you are creating the content for your detail page, be sure to think like a copywriter. You need to create copy that motivates people to buy your book instead of the many other competitive titles in the catalog. However, don't go overboard. Avoid creating a detail page that sounds like a sales pitch.

If a traditional publisher published your book, your publisher will transmit this information to Amazon. If you self-published, then you are responsible for transmitting this data. Even if your publisher is handling the details, I definitely recommend that you get involved in the process. By actively participating, you'll be able to better enhance the quality and content of what millions of Amazon customers view about your book.

If you have books listed on Amazon, verify that the detail page information is correct. To fix an error, scroll down to the bottom of your book's detail page and click the "Update Product Info" link in the Product Details section. A new page appears in which you can update information such as author name, title, edition, publication date, number of pages, and more. Remember to verify the accuracy of your listings on the Amazon sites outside your own country as well.

> **Tip**
>
> Amazon may be the most popular online bookstore in the world, but it definitely isn't the only one. Also verify and enhance your book's detail page on other sites including Barnes & Noble (**www.barnesandnoble.com**), Blackwell (**bookshop.blackwell.co.uk**), Booksamillion (**www.booksamillion.com**), Chapters Indigo (**www.chapters.indigo.ca**), Powell's Books (**www.powells.com**), and others.

Amazon Tags

In the Tags Customers Associate with This Product section of your book's detail page, you have two opportunities to make it easier for potential customers to find your book through tags: product tags and search tags. Tag your book with the terms people interested in your book's topic are most likely to search on. For additional ideas, review competitive books and their tags.

Search Inside! Program

To enable potential readers to browse through your book just as they would in a bookstore, Amazon created the Search Inside! Program. View your book's detail page to determine if your publisher has signed up for the Search Inside! program. All participating books have the Search Inside logo placed near the upper right corner of the book image. In addition to viewing the front and back covers, table of content, index, and excerpt, there is a text box for searching inside the book. Site visitors can't read your entire book, but they can view the pages related to a specific keyword to see if your book is right for them.

> **Tip**
>
> Look Inside the Book was an older Amazon search program that's no longer available, even though many books still use this program.

If you hold the rights to your book, you can sign up for Search Inside! on your own. If you don't hold the rights, work through your publisher to participate.

The search functionality will become active within three to five weeks if you submit your book electronically. If you submit a physical book, it can take up to eight weeks. There is no charge for this service. To learn more, visit **www.amazon.com/publishers**.

Encouraging Others to Review Your Book

Positive reader reviews generate sales. In order to increase the number of reviews for your book, politely encourage the following to write an Amazon book review:

- Readers who send you fan mail
- Participants at your lectures, readings, or book signings
- Individuals who provided book testimonials and endorsements

Tip	Some authors offer reviewers a "thank you" such as a special report, discount, or other product as an incentive to review their books. To remain ethical, be sure not to push for five-star reviews or tie the reward to a positive review. In general, I prefer just to ask for reviews without any mention of a reward for doing so.

Regardless of how great your book is, you'll eventually receive a bad review unless you're extremely lucky. Amazon won't remove these reviews unless they're obscene, defamatory, or violate their rules and regulations in some way. The best thing to do is just ignore the bad reviews and concentrate on getting more reviews to balance them. Most people can see through reviews that appear mean-spirited or unfair and won't hold them against you.

Web-Savvy in Action	Quincy is the author of a book on careers in the music industry. When he views his book's Amazon detail page for the first time, he discovers there is little information. Working with the publicist his publisher assigned to his book, Quincy provides additional content to help inform and interest potential readers in his book.
	Quincy also notices that he doesn't have any reviews yet. To remedy this situation, he starts asking people who say they enjoyed his book to post a review. Although not everyone responds to his request, several readers do write positive book reviews, which aid his promotional efforts.

Creating an Amazon Profile

Create a content-rich profile to let potential readers know more about you and your books.

Your Amazon Profile

Amazon enables you to create a user profile that includes a bio, photo, email address, and website link. Information from your profile appears whenever you post information on the site, such as a book review, Listmania! list, or So You'd Like to … guide. By carefully choosing the content in your profile, you can generate interest in your own books as well as drive traffic to your website.

Tip	Amazon also offers something called a Real Name™ attribution, enabling you to verify that you're using your real name in your Amazon profile and related content. Amazon uses information from your registered credit card to verify your real name.

AmazonConnect

AmazonConnect (**www.amazon.com/connect**) is a free program that fosters direct communication between authors and their readers. With AmazonConnect, you can add a list of your books to your profile page as well as create a blog on which you can post messages to your readers. Your blog appears on your book detail page as well as on your profile page. Note that you must validate your credentials with your publisher before you're allowed to post messages as the official author of a book.

In addition to posting directly to your Amazon blog, you can also incorporate content from external blogs. To do so, select Add RSS Feed from the Author Menu within Connect.

Web-Savvy in Action

Sebastian is the author of a medical thriller and wants to get as much publicity as possible for his new book on Amazon. He signs up for the AmazonConnect program and creates a profile that describes his book in detail, includes a recent photo, and provides a link to his website where readers can listen to an audio excerpt. Sebastian also creates an AmazonConnect blog, where he regularly posts messages related to his book and fans of medical thrillers in general.

▸ See chapter 3, "Promoting Your Book with a Blog"

Promoting Your Book on Amazon

Here are four other ideas for promoting your book on Amazon.

Listmania! Lists

Listmania! enables you to create a list of books or other products in the Amazon catalog that relate to a specific topic. Listmania! is a good promotional opportunity because Amazon prominently displays these lists throughout its site whenever someone searches for products related to the topic of your list. Each list also includes the name of the list author and a link to your profile. You can create as many lists as you want, so get creative and create several that relate to your subject area.

For example, to promote my PowerPoint book I created a Listmania! list titled "Ten Top Tools for the PowerPoint Power User" that lists ten items, including my own PowerPoint book, of interest to a PowerPoint power user.

So You'd Like to … Guides

So You'd Like to … guides are similar to Listmania! lists, but they take on the format of a how-to guide instead of a simple list. With a guide, you can offer advice on your area of expertise, incorporating recommended items for sale on Amazon such as your book. A guide can provide step-by-step instructions and can have headings. The word limit is 1,500 words with a minimum of 100 words. Look at several guides to get a feel for how you can use this tool to your advantage.

Paid Placements

If you're already selling your books through Amazon, consider the Paid Placements program (**www.amazon.com/coop**) to promote your work further.

This program, also called the Buy X, Get Y Program, or BXGY, enables you to piggyback off the success of bestselling titles that share your same niche audience. To find potential partners, look at the detail page of target books to see if there is a Best Value box listed. In this box, the target title is paired with another book available at a 5 percent discount. The existence of a Best Value box means that the target title has already been selected for a paid placement. If a similar box titled "Better Together" is listed, don't worry. This is part of an automated pairing program and isn't the same as a paid placement.

The Paid Placement program is rarely your first marketing effort on Amazon because of its cost, but can be valuable when paired with the right partner book.

Complementary Book and Product Reviews

By writing reviews of complementary books and products that target your audience, you can generate reader interest in your own books. Be sure to set up a profile that includes your website before entering your reviews so people who read them can find you.

Web-Savvy in Action	Arabella is the author of a home decorating book targeting the urban lifestyle. To promote her book, she creates several So You'd Like to … guides and Listmania! lists that cover topics of interest to her audience. She includes her own book on each list, but also incorporates useful decorating information that appeals to her target readers. Her lists appear on numerous pages in the Amazon catalog as well as on search engines such as Google, which gives her a lot of added exposure.

Other Ways to Make Money on Amazon

Here are four other ideas for making money on Amazon.

Amazon Upgrade

If you participate in the Search Inside! program, Amazon offers an additional revenue opportunity at no cost to publishers. With Amazon Upgrade, customers who purchase a physical copy of your book have the option of also purchasing online access at an additional charge. To learn more, visit **www.amazon.com/publishers**.

Amazon Marketplace

Amazon Marketplace (**www.amazon.com/marketplace**) is another option for selling your books, both new and used. With Marketplace, you pay a small commission and transaction fee only when you sell something. When someone makes a purchase, you ship the book directly to your customer. Amazon pays you every two weeks through its Amazon Payments system. One option to consider is the Pro Merchant Subscription service. With Pro Merchant, the transaction fee is waived, you have access to Inventory Loader for faster loading of multiple items, and you can list unlimited items. The Pro Merchant service carries a monthly fee, however, so it's most useful to volume sellers.

An important thing to note is that unless you sign up for the Pro Merchant service you can sell through Amazon Marketplace only if your book is already listed on the Amazon website. Why would you want to sell through Marketplace if you're already on Amazon? There are two reasons. You can sell used or returned books, and you could potentially make a higher profit on new books that you already possess.

Amazon Shorts

Amazon Shorts (**www.amazon.com/shorts**) enables published authors with at least one book currently for sale on Amazon to sell short works between 2,000 and 10,000 words as digital downloads priced at $0.49. Because of the low sales price, Amazon Shorts is probably best suited for short content designed to promote your career instead of a viable way to sell ebooks on Amazon. One example would be for a fiction writer to sell related short stories to help gain visibility for a published novel.

Amazon Honor System

If you'd like to accept donations on your site, you can easily do so with the Amazon Honor System (**www.amazon.com/honorsystem**). There is no fee to join the program, but Amazon takes a small commission and transaction fee for each donation you receive. Currently a U.S. credit card and checking account are required to participate.

Making Money with Amazon Associates

In addition to profiting from direct book sales on Amazon, you can also make money by referring sales to Amazon.

Amazon Associates Overview

Amazon Associates (**www.amazon.com/associates**) is Amazon's affiliate program. When you place a link on your website or blog to an item for sale on Amazon, you receive a referral fee on any purchases site visitors make after clicking the link. You can incorporate a variety of text links, banners, search boxes, and graphics on your site that all lead visitors to Amazon to purchase your recommended items. These include links to specific products as well as product categories.

One of the most common ways authors use the Associates program is to provide links to their book's detail page on the Amazon website. You can also make money by recommending complementary books and products.

In general, it's more effective to provide real content about the items you recommend, or write reviews of these items, than simply to provide a list of items. It usually takes some experimentation to determine how best to incorporate the Associates program into your site's content. By reviewing your Associates reports, you can see what does and doesn't work and make modifications from there.

If you want to customize the use of the Amazon Associates program on your site without the need for programming skills, check out one of the many third-party tools that can simplify and automate the process. One option to consider is Associate-O-Matic (**www.associate-o-matic.com**).

Amazon Web Services

Amazon Web Services (**www.amazon.com/webservices**) enables you to integrate further with the data in the Amazon catalog, creating a more customized experience for your site visitors, and hopefully, generating more income for you as an Amazon associate. If you have programming skills, or are willing to hire someone who does, sign up for a free Amazon Web Services account to gain access to this technology.

FeedBurner and Amazon Associates

If you use FeedBurner (**www.feedburner.com**) to generate your blog feed, you can automatically insert your Amazon Associates ID into any Amazon link in your feed using the Amazon ID Burner feature. Just enter your Associates ID in the specified field, activate, and you're ready to go.

Associates and Typepad

Integrating Amazon Associates links into your blog is easy with TypePad (**www.typepad.com**). If you recommend book and music choices on your blog, such as your own books, you can automatically embed your Amazon Associates ID in those links. In addition, you can post a link to your Amazon wish list.

**Web-Savvy
in Action**

Logan is the author of several historical novels set in Charleston, South Carolina. He joins Amazon Associates and places links for each of his books on his website, generating commissions whenever a site visitor clicks a link and buys one of his books on the Amazon site.

In addition, Logan creates a resources section on his site that offers original content about the history of Charleston, links to relevant websites, and reviews of books on Charleston and local history. In this section, he incorporates Amazon text and product links so he receives commissions on purchases of these related books as well.

▸ See chapter 9, "Promoting Your Book with Online Advertising," Generating Advertising Revenue

Tracking Your Success

As you start to sell books on Amazon, you'll want to track your results and make modifications to your marketing campaign as needed.

Analyzing Your Sales Rank

When you have a book for sale on Amazon, refer to your sales rank to see how your sales are progressing. Amazon updates the rank on an hourly basis. The lower the number, the more the book is selling. Although your sales rank is an important number, don't let a high number disappoint you.

If your book is on a specialized topic, it's unlikely to have a very good rank. Only widely publicized books on general interest topics normally generate very good sales ranks. In general, you should compare your sales rank with your competitors, not with today's hottest, bestselling books.

Also, check out the following websites that help you analyze your Amazon sales rank as well as that of competitive titles: Charteous (**charteo.us**) and TitleZ (**www.titlez.com**).

If you're in the planning stages of writing a book or creating a book proposal, searching by keyword can give you helpful clues on the current popularity of specific topics.

Tip

Amazon sales rank is just one way to determine the sales success of a book. Some books, particularly self-published books, generate a majority of their sales online on sites such as Amazon. Other books sell very well through bookstores, a publisher's own website, book clubs, and other bulk distribution methods that aren't reflected on Amazon.

Amazon Promotion Step-by-Step

Amazon offers authors a multitude of sales and promotional opportunities. Here's your step-by-step "to do" list:

- ☐ Get your book listed on Amazon, either through your publisher or through your own efforts if you self-published

- ☐ Review and update your book's detail page with content that encourages sales

- ☐ Sign up for the Amazon Associates program if you have books available on Amazon and want to earn commission on their sale from your website

- ☐ Sign up for the Search Inside! program or request that your publisher do so

- ☐ Encourage others to review your book on Amazon

- ☐ Tag your book's content to make it easier for potential readers to find it

- ☐ Create an Amazon Profile that showcases your background

- ☐ Sign up for AmazonConnect and use it to connect with your audience

- ☐ Create Listmania! lists and So You'd Like to … guides related to your book

- ☐ Review complementary books and products (with the right profile, readers can find your books, too)

- ☐ Consider Amazon's many other programs and services to see if they match your goals and could help generate more revenue or publicity

- ☐ Track your sales rank, compare it to similar titles, and make adjustments to your Amazon campaign if necessary

9

Promoting Your Book
with Online Advertising

Purchasing paid advertising shouldn't be the first component in your online marketing campaign, but it can be a lucrative option for many authors. Paid advertising works best for nonfiction authors, particularly those who also consult, speak, and sell supplemental products. Some novelists, however, are now experimenting with online advertising as well.

The options for paid advertising are varied. You can advertise on search engine result pages, websites, ezines, blogs, feeds, podcasts, and more. In addition, you can generate your own advertising revenue by accepting ads on your content.

Quick Fact	U.S. online advertising will continue steady growth over the next few years, eventually reaching $18.9 billion in 2010. Search engine advertising will generate more revenue than standard display advertising by 2010. Rich media spending will grow to $3.5 billion and streaming media will grow to $943 million by 2010. —*Source: JupiterResearch*

Getting Ready to Advertise Online

As with any other aspect of your online marketing campaign, you need to educate yourself about online advertising and then create an action plan.

Creating a Niche Advertising Plan

Before you spend any money on paid advertising, establish goals and determine what you want to achieve from your advertising purchases. Ask yourself these questions:

- Who is your audience?

- What do you want your prospects to do (for example, buy your book, purchase supplemental products, attend your seminars, hire you for your consulting services, and so forth)?
- What sites do your target prospects visit?
- What ezines and blogs does your audience read?
- Where are your competitors advertising?
- What keywords would potential customers search on to find what you're selling?

Online Advertising Basics

You can advertise online in many ways. Pay-per-click (PPC) advertising is one of the most popular forms of online advertising available today. Google AdWords, Yahoo! Search Marketing, and Microsoft adCenter all offer PPC programs with affordable rates. Although each PPC program differs slightly, they all use a similar approach:

1. As an advertiser, you create a short text ad that includes a link to a target page on your website called a landing page.
2. You choose which keywords you want to target and bid on these words, indicating how much you are willing to pay for a click through to your site.
3. Your ad appears on search engine result pages, websites, or blogs with content relevant to your ad and selected keywords.
4. You pay every time a visitor clicks your ad to go to your site. You aren't charged if your ad appears on a page, but isn't clicked. This is called a cost-per-click (CPC) pricing model.

Tip

Although PPC advertising isn't difficult, a detailed analysis of the do's and don'ts of this form of online advertising is beyond the scope of this book. If you're interested in pursuing PPC opportunities, you should research the most popular PPC programs (Google, Yahoo!, and Microsoft), take any relevant online training they offer, and then compare programs to determine which one best suits your individual needs. Start with one program, and then modify or expand your advertising plan as required.

In addition to PPC advertising, you can also purchase ads directly from websites, blogs, and ezines that attract your target audience.

Online Copywriting Basics

Small text ads appear deceptively simple to write. Here are some tips for creating ads that generate positive results:

- Read the guidelines for creating ads for a specific PPC program and follow them.
- Use your keywords in your ad title.

- Include a call to action in your ad, such as a free offer or discount, but don't create an ad filled with sales hype.
- Create a solid landing page, that is, the page visitors land on when they click your ad. Your landing page could be your website's homepage, or better, a special page dedicated to achieving your target goal.
- Try several versions of your ad to determine which one generates the best results.
- Review your ads periodically and modify your approach as needed.

Advertising Online

With an idea in mind of how you'd like to advertise, it's time to do an analysis of the sites and services that offer advertising opportunities.

Quick Fact	Search engine marketing will grow to $11.6 billion by 2010. Other new advertising channels will also draw interest and spending, with 64 percent of surveyed marketers interested in advertising on blogs, 57 percent through RSS, and 52 percent on mobile devices, including phones and PDAs. —*Source: US Online Marketing Forecast: 2005 To 2010, Forrester Research, Inc., 2005*

Google AdWords

Google AdWords (**adwords.google.com**) is one of the most popular PPC advertising programs available. AdWords enables you to display your text ads on Google search result pages, sites throughout the Google Network, and partner sites such as About, AOL, Ask.com, Food Network, Shopping.com, and The New York Times. The Google Network refers to the many websites and blogs that display Google ads through participation in the Google AdSense (**www.google.com/adsense**) program. Later in this chapter, you'll learn how to generate revenue by displaying other advertisers' ads on your own site.

Before getting started with AdWords, be sure to work through the lessons provided in the Google AdWords Learning Center (**www.google.com/adwords/learningcenter**). This provides an excellent overview of how to get the most out of AdWords as well as a good introduction to PPC advertising in general.

One of the advantages of the AdWords program is that you're able to bid specific amounts for the keywords you target so you're always in control of your total advertising expense, even if you can't control how many people actually click on your ads. For example, you can set a daily AdWords budget that the system won't exceed.

AdWords users should sign up for a free Google Analytics (**www.google.com/analytics**) account. Google Analytics enables you to track and analyze all of your online advertising and marketing campaigns including AdWords and affiliate campaigns. It also offers numerous other reporting and analysis tools useful to anyone with an ecommerce website.

Web-Savvy in Action

Javier is a golf pro and the author of a book and video series for beginning golfers. To promote his products, Javier decides to create a PPC advertising campaign. After performing some keyword research, he chooses "golf video," "golf instruction," and "beginning golf" as his target keyword phrases. He creates an ad that he feels his target prospects will be motivated to click, designs a solid landing page that promotes his book and video series, and begins an initial campaign based on his target budget. Over time, Javier analyzes the results of his campaign and modifies his ads and keywords to generate the most revenue.

Yahoo! Search Marketing

Yahoo! Search Marketing (**searchmarketing.yahoo.com**) offers a PPC advertising program called Sponsored Search, enabling you to place your ads in search results on Yahoo! and partner sites including eBay, WebMD, and hundreds of online newspapers. Like AdWords, you bid for specific keywords and set your own budget. Be sure to watch the online demo to view Sponsored Search in action.

In addition, Yahoo! ads also appear on sites that are part of the Yahoo! Publisher Network (**publisher.yahoo.com**), which is similar to Google AdSense.

Microsoft adCenter

Microsoft adCenter (**adcenter.microsoft.com**) enables you to advertise on MSN, Live Search, MSN Mobile, and other Microsoft sites as well as on partner sites including Facebook, Digg, and CNBC.com. Options include keyword search, display, and rich media advertising.

Ezines Advertising

Ezines reach a targeted audience interested in a specific topic and frequently offer advertising at reasonable rates. Advertising in tightly targeted ezines can be a cost-effective way to promote your book. Review the subscriber numbers and advertising rates for the ezines targeting the audience that most closely matches your own to determine appropriate candidates for advertising. If you publish your own ezine, consider ad exchanges, article exchanges, or contributing articles to other ezines as other effective ways to promote.

▶ See chapter 6, "Promoting Your Book with an Ezine"

Web-Savvy in Action

Coco is the author of a traditionally published book on healthy family cooking who also creates a series of self-published ebooks on related topics. She identifies websites, ezines, and blogs that serve her target audience—including cooking, parenting, and women's sites—and contributes articles and content to them whenever possible.

To expand her visibility within this market, she decides to try a test advertising campaign. Coco picks the top five websites, blogs, and ezines that reach her audience and places ads on them, including banner and text ads. During her initial advertising campaign, Coco analyzes the response on each ad. She discovers that one website and one ezine generate the majority of additional sales and now focuses her entire advertising budget on these two proven sources.

Website Advertising

In addition to joining advertising programs that cover multiple websites, you should also look into individual advertising opportunities on high-traffic sites that attract your target audience. If you did the research recommended in previous chapters, you should already have a list of sites that meet these qualifications, yet aren't direct competitors. Visit theses sites again to learn more about any advertising and sponsorship opportunities they offer. In many cases, sites post their advertising rates online.

Generating Advertising Revenue

In addition to paying to advertise your books, products, and services, you can also generate advertising revenue from your own content, such as your website, blog, feed, and podcast.

Unless your site receives heavy traffic you probably won't make a fortune from advertising revenue, but it can help pay for the cost of hosting and other online services.

Tip

It's important to determine when advertising on your website is and isn't appropriate, which is a judgment call for most authors. Personally, I don't recommend using advertising on pages designed to showcase your books, writing portfolio, background, and services, but they can work nicely on resource or informational pages. Advertising also works well on informational sites you create on your area of expertise as well as on blogs, feeds, and podcasts.

▶ See chapter 3, "Promoting Your Book with a Blog," Accepting Advertising on Your Blog

▶ See chapter 4, "Promoting Your Book with a Feed," Profiting from Your Feed

▶ See chapter 5, "Promoting Your Book with a Podcast," Profiting from Your Podcast

Advertising Revenue with Google AdSense

One of the easiest ways to start generating advertising revenue from your website or blog is to join Google AdSense (**www.google.com/adsense**). With Google AdSense, you display the ads created by advertisers participating in the Google AdWords program described earlier. In essence, your site becomes part of the Google Network. Google AdSense also offers advertising options for feeds and mobile content.

To participate, sign up for a free AdSense account, specify the format for your ads, and insert the automatically generated HTML code into your web pages. This isn't difficult; anyone with basic HTML knowledge should be able to copy and paste the code. Because the ads are contextual, their content relates directly to the content of your web page. For example, if your page contains information about travel to London, the AdSense ads pertain to this same topic. When visitors click an ad, you generate revenue under the revenue-per-click model.

To learn more about AdSense and discover some tricks about getting the most from the program, watch the demos available at **www.google.com/support/adsense**.

The Google AdSense website clearly points out the do's and don'ts of using AdSense (**www.google.com/adsense/policies**). Here are few reminders:

- Don't click your own ads. This unfairly inflates your AdSense revenue and Google knows when you participate in click fraud. So don't.
- Avoid directly asking site visitors to click your AdSense ads. They see them and click them if they're interested.
- Don't change the AdSense code. This includes trying to modify the code to open ads in a new page. If you want to modify the colors and format, you should do so on the Google AdSense site, which offers multiple options.
- Do place AdSense code only on content pages, not on error pages or thank-you pages. AdSense needs real content to deliver context-relevant ads.

Advertising Revenue with Yahoo! Publisher Network

Yahoo! Publisher Network (**publisher.yahoo.com**) is a revenue-per-click (RPC) advertising opportunity for website publishers that's tied to ads from Yahoo! Search Marketing. Similar to AdSense, Yahoo! Publisher Network enables you to specify the look and layout of your ads and generate HTML code to insert on your web pages. When visitors click an ad, you earn money. If you publish your blog with WordPress or Moveable Type, you can also insert ads into your feed.

Affiliate Marketing Revenue

Affiliate marketing programs enable you to receive commissions by referring your site visitors to other sites where they can make purchases. One of the most popular affiliate programs in the book publishing community is the Amazon Associates program (**www.amazon.com/associates**).

With Amazon Associates, you can provide links from your site to any product available on Amazon.com, such as books you have written or other products you recommend. You're paid a commission when a site visitor clicks the link on your site and purchases the item.

Amazon may be one of the largest affiliate programs, but it certainly isn't the only one. Seeking out individual affiliate programs for products that target your exact audience is also a good idea.

If you want to recommend numerous products, look into affiliate sites that enable you to sign up as an affiliate with multiple companies under a single account. Some to consider:

- ClickBank (**www.clickbank.com**)
- clixGalore (**www.clixgalore.com**)
- Commission Junction (**www.cj.com**)
- LinkShare (**www.linkshare.com**)

Although you can make money as an affiliate, it's important not to go overboard. Try to limit your affiliate referrals to products you already use or you believe truly provide value to your site visitors.

▶ See chapter 8, "Selling and Promoting Your Book on Amazon.com," Making Money with Amazon Associates

▶ See chapter 15, "Twelve More Ways to Promote Your Book Online," Create Your Own Affiliate Program

Web-Savvy in Action

Pierre is the author of a series of books on web design whose website includes an extensive collection of web resources. He decides to generate additional income by placing AdSense ads on these resource pages.

In addition, Pierre joins several affiliate programs and includes affiliate links to other products he recommends such as software, hosting services, clip art libraries, and more.

Other Revenue-Generating Ideas

Here are six other ideas for generating advertising revenue from your sites and content:

- **AdBrite (www.adbrite.com).** An Internet ad marketplace that enables you to set your price for advertising and offers a 75 percent revenue share.
- **Burst Media (www.burstmedia.com).** An advertising network for sites with a minimum of 5,000 page views per month.
- **Chitika (www.chitika.com).** Offers the Premium Ads program that targets to your search engine traffic as well as the eMiniMalls shopping program.
- **CrispAds (www.crispads.com).** A blog advertising network that offers keyword-based text ads and category-based graphic ads with a 70 percent revenue share.
- **Shopzilla (publisher.shopzilla.com).** Earn revenue by displaying sponsored shopping content on your site.
- **Text Link Ads (www.text-link-ads.com).** Enables you to sell context-relevant text ads on your site.

Remember not to go overboard with advertising options. Choose a few of the most profitable options and work with those rather than overloading your content site with ads.

Online Advertising Step-by-Step

Although online advertising is rarely your first option in online book promotion, it can achieve impressive results for the right book. Here's your step-by-step "to do" list:

- ☐ Research online advertising and verify that you understand the basic concepts

- ☐ Determine whether your books or products are a good match for online advertising

- ☐ Select one pay-per-click advertising program to start (such as Google AdWords, Yahoo! Search Marketing, or Microsoft adCenter) and develop a campaign for that program; consider others only after evaluating your first choice

- ☐ Learn about online copywriting and create concise text ads that generate results

- ☐ Research and pursue targeted advertising on websites, blogs, and ezines, if this is appropriate for your book

- ☐ Select and implement one revenue-per-click advertising program (such as Google AdSense or Yahoo! Publisher Network) if you want to generate revenue from your content pages

- ☐ Research and sign up for relevant affiliate marketing programs if you want to generate revenue by recommending related products

10

Promoting Your Book with Audio and Video

Using audio and video as informational, sales, and promotional tools offers some distinct advantages for authors looking to promote their books with a creative edge. For example:

- Site visitors are far more likely to remember a message conveyed through audio, video, *and* text than a message conveyed through text alone.
- Anything new and different draws more attention than promotions that are similar to everything else on the Internet. For example, ten years ago, just having a website was enough to draw an audience, but now websites are everywhere. Today, you need something unique to attract attention.
- Using new technologies makes you appear current and cutting edge.

Quick Fact	More than 100 million users consume online digital media (streams and downloads) in the U.S. in a month, which represents almost 60 percent of the U.S. online population (97.5 million computers). —*Source: comScore Networks*

Promoting with Audio

The simple use of audio can have a positive impact on your ability to reach and connect with your audience. This section discusses the use of streaming audio, radio, and teleseminars. Podcasting, another form of audio promotion, is covered in Chapter 5, "Promoting Your Book with a Podcast."

Streaming Website Audio

Streaming audio is audio that plays directly from the web. The advantage of streaming audio is that it streams, or downloads as it plays, so that you don't have to wait for a large file to download. Streaming audio isn't just for websites. You can also use this technology with blogs and ezines.

If you think that you can reach your target audience through the spoken word, consider recording an audio message. For example, you may want to post a website greeting, introduce the topic of a book you published, or read a passage from a work of fiction or poetry. One technique to avoid, however, is having your audio message play automatically as soon as visitors reach your website. Studies show that automated audio messages tend to annoy rather than entertain most site visitors. For best results, let your site visitors choose to listen to your audio by clicking a simple button.

Tip	In addition to streaming audio directly from your website, another option to consider is creating audio seminars to sell as either a downloadable MP3 or audio CD.

Some streaming audio software and services to check out include:

- **AudioAcrobat (www.audioacrobat.com)**. Records, hosts, and streams website audio for a monthly fee. Also includes video streaming and podcasting features. Offers a free 30-day trial.
- **AudioGenerator (www.audiogenerator.com)**. An audio recording, hosting, and streaming service that charges a monthly fee with unlimited audio messages. Free 21-day trial.
- **Flash Audio Wizard (www.flashaudiowizard.com)**. Software program that enables you to record and stream audio on your website. One-time download fee with no monthly fees.
- **Gabcast (www.gabcast.com)**. Enables you to create free audio greetings for your website or blog. Also offers podcasting services.

Web-Savvy in Action	Midori is a professional organizer who has published several books on her specialty. She also offers organizing seminars and consulting services. To better connect with her audience, she records and posts a 15-minute mini-seminar that's available as free streaming audio on her website. In addition, she uses streaming audio to post customer testimonials on her site. In these testimonials, previous and existing customers praise the way Midori's books, seminars, and consulting have helped them get organized and save time, money, and frustration.

Radio Tours

Another way to use audio as a promotional tool is to create your own radio tour. Radio has an advantage over traditional book tours in that you can reach a wider audience much more quickly with radio shows than you can by visiting physical bookstores. Thousands of potential shows, including hundreds of large audience shows, are looking for guests. An added bonus is that you can usually participate from the comfort of your own home rather than from a studio.

Satellite radio is another option for book authors looking to promote via radio. Hosting your own podcast, or being interviewed on an existing podcast, is yet another variation.

Quick Fact	The U.S. satellite radio market will grow to 55 million units in 2010. —*Source: JupiterResearch*

Some good resources on radio tours include:

- **Annie Jennings PR (www.anniejenningspr.com).** Coordinates a top market radio campaign for book authors, among other services.
- **Radio Publicity (www.radiopublicity.com).** Sells a database of more than 1,000 major talk radio shows as well as provides other information on radio publicity.
- **The Readers Radio Network (www.readersradionetwork.com).** Produces radio-based virtual book tours.
- **Radio-TV Interview Report (www.rtir.com).** A fee-based directory of authors and experts available for radio and TV interviews.

Web-Savvy in Action	Toby is a champion athlete who overcame serious injuries from a car accident to excel again at his sport. He chronicles his inspirational story in a book and wants to share this story with as many people as possible. Toby enjoys public speaking and plans to launch a career as a motivational speaker. To promote both his book and his speaking career, he arranges a nationwide radio publicity tour by advertising in radio guest directories as well as pitching shows directly.

▶ See Chapter 5, "Promoting Your Book with a Podcast"

Teleseminars

Conducting your own teleseminars, or being a guest participant on someone else's teleseminar, helps promote your book as well as generate income. Although some authors offer free teleseminars to interest prospective clients, this works best for promoting high-priced consulting or coaching services in addition to your book. For other authors, creating a teleseminar based on the topic of your book provides an additional revenue stream.

If hosting a teleseminar sounds like a good match for your background, compare prices at companies that offer teleseminar services, including access to telephone bridge lines, call recording, transcripts, toll-free numbers, seminar management, and more. Some choices to consider include:

- Great Teleseminars (**www.greatteleseminars.com**)
- Rentabridge.com (**www.rentabridge.com**)
- Telebridge (**www.telebridge.com**)
- TeleConferenceLine.com (**www.teleconferenceline.com**)

Here are some tips for teleseminar success:

- Before creating your own teleseminar, attend a few hosted by others to get a feel for how they work. To find a teleseminar that interests you, do a web search on "teleseminar" or check out Seminar Announcer (**www.seminarannouncer.com**) for free and fee options. You can also learn about teleseminars from ezines, blogs, and social networking sites. I receive teleseminar invitations almost weekly on Facebook.

- Carefully consider your needs before choosing a teleseminar service or renting a telephone bridge line. How many participants do you anticipate? Do you want to record your call? Do you want to use a toll or toll-free number? Do you plan to charge for your teleseminar or offer it free? Knowing the answers to these questions helps you make the right choice based on your budget and requirements.

- To generate even more revenue, record your teleseminars and market the audio on your website as a downloadable MP3 or audio CD. Selling teleseminar transcripts is another option. Alternatively, you can skip the teleseminar and just record an audio CD or MP3 that you can sell.

- To promote your teleseminar, announce it on your website, blog, and ezine as well as on other complementary sites and publications. In addition, you can list your teleseminar on websites such as Seminar Announcer.

Web-Savvy in Action

Madison is a certified financial planner and the author of a book on money management for women. Although she has traveled around the country presenting seminars on her area of expertise, she would like to spend more time at home with her family. To accomplish this, she decides to present the material from her live seminars as a teleseminar. Madison develops a large mailing list for her ezine and promotes her new teleseminars extensively in each ezine issue as well as on her website. As an added revenue stream, she records each teleseminar and sells downloadable MP3s and audio CDs from her website.

Promoting with Video

Enabling your audience to view something, either you discussing your book or a short video related to your book's topic, is another way to connect with readers.

Quick Fact	In March 2008, nearly 74 percent of the entire U.S. Internet audience viewed online videos, for a total of 11.5 billion online video views. —*Source: comScore*

Streaming Website Video

A streaming video message is a worthwhile option to consider. You can post a video clip you already have, such as one of you presenting, speaking, or doing something related to your specialty. Or if you have a camcorder or webcam, you can record your own video message such as a welcome message or introduction to your book. Some other interesting ideas include:

- A travel guidebook author could post a short travel video of a frequently covered destination
- A cookbook author could record a video of cooking techniques
- A ski journalist might create a video illustrating some of the ski techniques discussed in his book

Tip	Remember that video takes up bandwidth, so focus on creating short clips that serve as a marketing tool rather than long informational videos.

A variety of software and hosting options are available for streaming website video:

- Adobe Visual Communicator (**www.adobe.com/products/visualcommunicator**)
- Adobe Vlog It! (**www.adobe.com/products/vlogit**)
- AudioAcrobat (**www.audioacrobat.com**)
- Camtix Video (**www.camtix.com**)
- SWiSH Video3 (**www.swishzone.com**)
- Webmaster Media Maker: Streaming Video (**www.webmastermediamaker.com**)

Tip	If you're not ready to add video to your website or blog, you can still enhance its visual appeal by incorporating photos and images.

▶ See Chapter 1, "Promoting your Book with a Website," Getting Graphic

Web-Savvy in Action	Morris is a ski instructor and the author of a book on advanced ski techniques. To promote both his book as well as his ski seminars, he records several brief video skiing lessons and streams these videos on his website. By heavily promoting his free online skiing lessons, he draws targeted traffic to his website with potential interest in his book or ski seminars.

Video Book Trailers

Book videos—also known as book trailers, book teasers, or book presenters—are short web videos, similar to movie trailers, designed to promote a book. Book videos vary greatly in style, format, and concept, but are usually several minutes in length and serve a singular purpose—to convert video viewers into book buyers. Many book trailers are in a slideshow format with text, background music, and video transitions used to bring still images to life. Other book videos are more sophisticated, using actual video footage and even live actors to depict scenes in your book.

You can create your own book trailer using software such as:

- Adobe Flash (**www.adobe.com/products/flash**)
- Adobe Photoshop Elements (**www.adobe.com/products/photoshopelwin**)
- iMovie (**www.apple.com/ilife/imovie**)
- Microsoft Photo Story
  (**www.microsoft.com/windowsxp/using/digitalphotography/ photostory/default.mspx**)

Another option is to create a PowerPoint presentation and convert it to a web video using a program such as Camtasia Studio (**www.camtasiastudio.com**). If you're on a budget, FlashSpring (**www.flashspring.com**) is another option.

Or, you can hire a production service to create a trailer for you such as AuthorBytes (**www.authorbytes.com**), Book Candy Studios (**www.bookcandystudios.com**), or COS Productions (**www.cosproductions.com**).

Tip	It takes a certain level of skill to develop your own book trailer. You don't need to be a programmer or artist, but you do need to be reasonably comfortable learning new software applications and have a flair for design to create a professional presentation. Otherwise, you're better off hiring someone to create your presentation if this is something you'd really like to publish on your site.
	If you're the do-it-yourself type or on a tight budget, you can learn more about creating your own trailer in my report *Video Book Buzz: Create a Book Video That Generates Publicity and Profits* (**www.websavvywriter.com**).

If you have the budget and want wider distribution, consider these other options:

- **BookstreamInc (www.bookstreaminc.com).** Produces author video interview clips called bookwraps. There's a choice of four different formats, including a deluxe bookwrap with a synopsis, author biography, excerpts, and review information.
- **Expanded Books (www.expandedbooks.com).** Produces book promotional videos viewable on Yahoo!, MSN, and other sites.
- **iReadNet (www.ireadnet.com).** Plans and produces video book tours for traditionally published books.

Web-Savvy in Action

Rafaella is the author of a romantic suspense novel who decides to promote her new book with a book trailer. She wants a professional look to her trailer, but she's on a budget. Because she developed solid PowerPoint skills in her previous corporate career, Rafaella is able to create a PowerPoint presentation that incorporates audio, video, and animation. She enhances her presentation in Camtasia Studio and converts it to a video trailer she uploads to YouTube and embeds on her website and blog. The trailer makes her book's characters and plot come alive, encouraging readers to purchase her book.

Screencasting

A screencast enables you to create online demos and tutorials and save them as a video or Flash movie. Although the most common use of a screencast is to demonstrate how to use a software program or website, there are also more creative ways to utilize this technology. Some examples include:

- Drawing on your computer screen with an online whiteboard or illustration tool
- Commenting on content you display on your computer screen, such as a photograph or illustration
- Displaying a video of yourself talking about your book while other multimedia content appears in the background, using picture-in-picture technology

Two screencasting tools to check out:

- **Camtasia Studio (www.camtasiastudio.com).** A full-featured screen recording and presentation application, Camtasia Studio enables you to create screencasts, online tutorials, demos, and other presentations and publish them in Flash and other formats for web, CD, or DVD use. Offers a free 30-day trial.
- **CamStudio (www.camstudio.org).** An open source software program that provides basic screencasting functionality at the right price—it's free.

Screencasting isn't just for creating free demos. You can also create online tutorials for which you charge a fee to access.

Web-Savvy in Action	Randy is the author of a book on drawing for beginners. As a promotional tool for his book, Randy creates two screencasts that are available for free viewing on his website and on YouTube and other video-sharing sites. The first is a tutorial demonstrating basic drawing skills using a simple whiteboard application. In the second, Randy presents a slideshow of his own illustrations commenting on specific drawing techniques that he discusses in more detail in his book.

Not only do these screencast videos provide valuable content for his audience, but they also demonstrate Randy's considerable illustration skills. Next, Randy is looking into creating a series of more in-depth paid tutorials as a supplemental income stream.

Promoting Your Video

Whether you create a live-action video, book trailer, or screencast, you need to make the most of your investment by ensuring it receives the largest number of viewers possible.

To gain visibility and increase sales, promote your video on:

- Video-sharing sites such as YouTube (**www.youtube.com**), Google Video (**video.google.com**), and Revver (**www.revver.com**)
- Social networking sites such as MySpace (**www.myspace.com**) and Facebook (**www.facebook.com**)
- Book-related sites such as Book Marketing Network (**bookmarket.ning.com**)
- Social bookmarking sites such as Digg (**www.digg.com**), StumbleUpon (**www.stumbleupon.com**), and del.icio.us (**del.icio.us**)
- Your website and blog
- Your signature file on every email you send
- Your press releases

Audio and Video Step-by-Step

When you have your basic website in place, enhancing it with audio and video can help entertain and inform your readers as well as increase sales. Here's your "to do" list of ideas to explore:

☐ Research audio and video and verify that you understand the basic concepts

☐ Determine technical requirements (hardware, software, and other services)

☐ Purchase a product or service that offers streaming audio if you feel that audio will help you connect with your audience

☐ Sign up with a radio campaign service or create your own radio tour

☐ Sign up with a teleseminar service, create your own teleseminar, or become a guest on someone else's teleseminar

☐ Purchase a product or services that offers streaming website video if your topic is suited to video promotion

☐ Create a video book trailer, either through a service or on your own (be sure to try any software before you buy it to make sure it's right for you)

☐ Sign up with a service that produces professional author video clips or video book tours if you feel this type of promotion would enhance your campaign

☐ Create a screencast, either as a promotional tool or as a tutorial you sell for profit

11

Promoting Your Book with Online Press Releases

All authors know that getting media exposure for their book is a good thing. A press release is a proven way of attracting media attention. Creating a release targeted for online distribution and publication can offer added advantages. For example, with online press releases you can:

- Reach the media and potentially earn media exposure in magazines, newspapers, and websites as well as on radio and television
- Reach your target audience directly through inclusion in online wire services, such as Google News, that the general public searches
- Increase your search engine visibility and ranking by optimizing your online releases with targeted keywords

Tip	If you published your book with a traditional publisher, check with your assigned publicist before issuing a book announcement release. This person may already have something planned for your book. Issuing releases for related products, services, and events that mention you as the author of your book shouldn't be a problem, however. If you self-published, creating your own book release is a necessity.

Online Press Release Basics

Here are some tips for creating an online press release that generates results:

- A press release isn't an advertisement or a sales letter. It's an announcement directed to the press and, in the case of an online release, to the public as well. That said, your release still should have some form of call to action, but definitely not an overt sales pitch.

- Use proper press release style and format. If you're not sure how to do this, refer to the website of the press release service you want to use. Most provide detailed instructions on how to format your release properly.

- The first few sentences of your release should spark an interest and encourage further reading. Studies indicate that the average journalist spends only a few seconds skimming a release before deciding whether to continue reading or move on.

- Optimize your release for search engines by including your targeted keywords in your title and several times throughout the release text. Don't overdo it, though.

- Link your target keywords to relevant pages on your website.

- Include one or two links to your website in your press release text, as anchor text.

- In addition to creating a release announcing your book, also consider creating some feature-style releases on topics related to your book.

- If possible, tie your press release to a current event.

- Include an image of your book's cover with your release as well as any related photos, such as an author photo.

- Consider including quotes in your releases, either a well-known individual offering a testimonial about your book or your own quote, which is particularly good for your feature-style releases.

Tip   Post an online media kit on your website that is easy for journalists to find.

▶ See chapter 1, "Promoting Your Book with a Website," Getting the Attention of the Media with an Online Media Kit

Distributing Your Online Press Release

Several choices exist for distributing your press release, ranging from full-service to free. When choosing a press distribution service, compare current pricing, features, and your target distribution areas.

Full-Service Press Release Distribution

Consider large newswires such as PR Newswire (**www.prnewswire.com**) and Business Wire (**www.businesswire.com**) only if your book's topic is of interest to a wide, general audience and you have a solid publicity budget. Their coverage is extensive, but it comes at a price. If you're interested in PR Newswire, be sure to check out their programs for small business and entrepreneurs.

Mid-Priced Press Release Distribution

If your budget is more modest (several hundred dollars or less), here are some other good options to consider:

- **eReleases (www.ereleases.com).** Includes national distribution through its partnership with PR Newswire.
- **PRWeb (www.prweb.com).** Offers several distribution options with staggered pricing for features such as social media visibility and SEO visibility.
- **Send2Press (www.send2press.com).** Provides multiple press release distribution options with varied pricing, target audiences, and features.

Free Press Release Distribution

If you're considering free press release distribution, remember the saying, "you get what you pay for." In general, free services focus on limited online distribution and don't provide sufficient coverage for a major media campaign. They can play a useful role, however, for secondary releases designed to achieve added search engine visibility.

- **PR.com (www.pr.com).** Offers free distribution to search engines and news sites such as Google News, Yahoo! Search, MSN, and more.
- **PRLog (www.prlog.org).** Provides the ability to include links, images, logos, tags, and keywords in your releases.
- **PressBox (www.pressbox.co.uk).** Free press distribution service based in the UK.

Creating a Social Media Press Release

Social media press releases combine the content of a traditional release with:

- Keywords that make your release easy to find on search engines
- Multimedia elements such as podcast, audio, video, and photo links
- Feeds and Technorati tags
- Buttons for readers to add to del.icio.us, Digg, and other social bookmarking sites

If you're interested in creating a social media press release, view the Shift Communications social media press release template (**www.shiftcomm.com/downloads/smr_v1.5.pdf**), which offers a simple approach to incorporating social media into your release. You don't have to use all the options of a social media release. You can pick and choose what works best for you and your book.

PRWeb (**www.prweb.com**) is a good choice for distributing a social media release on a modest budget. Posting your release directly on your website can also yield good results. For an example, see the social media release I created for my book *The Truth About Profiting from Social Networking* (**www.patricerutledge.com/socialnetworking/press-release**).

Tip	Another great way to gain media coverage is to sign up for a publicity leads service that sends you reporter requests for interview sources. Two to consider are Help a Reporter Out (**www.helpareporter.com**), which is free, and the fee-based PR Leads (**www.prleads.com**). To maintain a positive rapport with the media, respond only if your book is a good match with the reporter's request.

Tracking Your Online Press Release Success

After implementing an online press release campaign, you'll want to know how effective it was. Although the most obvious sign of success is an increase in revenue, you should also track your mentions on the web. To do so, set up alerts with Google Alerts (**www.google.com/alerts**) and Yahoo! Alerts (**alerts.yahoo.com**). You can set up alerts for your name, your company name, book titles, and anything else you want to track. Then when your search term appears online, you'll receive an email notification.

Web-Savvy in Action	Wally is an executive coach who just self-published a book on work/life balance for senior professionals. His goals are to develop his clientele, gain media coverage, and sell more books. To achieve this, he plans an online publicity campaign and writes three press releases to distribute at staggered times.
	The first is a book announcement timed for the release of his book. The other two are feature-style releases that also highlight his book and coaching services. Wally carefully constructs his releases to emphasize his target keyword phrase of "work/life balance" and includes extras such as links to his website, an image of his book cover, and a podcast.

Online Press Releases Step-by-Step

Here's a "to do" list that will help you get your book in the news:

☐ Plan an online press release campaign to promote your book, starting with a release to introduce your book and following with additional releases to keep your book in the news

☐ Select the most appropriate distribution service based on your requirements, audience, and budget

☐ Learn about social media press releases and consider creating one if this format is a good match for your book

☐ Distribute your release

☐ Post your press release to your website

☐ Track your success with Google Alerts and Yahoo! Alerts

☐ Join a publicity leads service and respond to relevant requests

12

Promoting Your Book with Article Marketing

Creating a series of short articles related to your book's subject matter and making these articles available for free reprint to other websites and ezines is another solid online marketing technique. There are numerous advantages to article marketing, particularly the ability to generate publicity across the web and drive traffic to your site.

By including a resource box at the end of your articles, readers can go to your website to learn more about you, and hopefully, purchase your book. In general, article marketing works better for authors of nonfiction how-to books than it does for authors of fiction, narrative nonfiction, and books on highly specialized topics.

Focused Content for Maximum Results

If you decide that article marketing is a technique worth pursuing, choose your article topics carefully and create focused content for maximum results. Here are some tips:

- Remember that you're writing a how-to article, not a press release or a sales letter. Readers respond best to an article that provides valuable content they can use instead of an article that's an advertisement in disguise.
- Aim to write articles that are between 250 and 750 words in length.
- For better search engine placement, use your target keywords in your title and in your text.
- Focus your article on one specific topic instead of trying to cover multiple topics in one article.
- Tip and list articles work well for article marketing.

The Right Resource Box

A resource box is the author bio that appears at the end of your article. Here are some tips for making the most of these few sentences:

- Keep it short. This isn't the time for a comprehensive biography. Focus on who you are and what you do in context with the article you wrote.
- Keep it professional. Resource boxes that make wild claims or promote too aggressively don't generate the results you want.
- Include a call to action. You wrote your article for a reason, that is, to get readers to take a specific action, such as visiting your website for more information on your book and services or signing up for your ezine.
- Include a link to your website in this format: http://www.websavvywriter.com.
- Offer a freebie such as a special report, sample chapter, or ecourse to provide an added incentive for readers to respond.
- Include keywords in an anchored text link somewhere in your resource box.

Submitting Your Articles

Once you've written several targeted articles, it's time to submit them to article directories. Hundreds of directories, as well as announcement lists, offer free articles for reprint. Some offer general interest articles on a variety of topics. Others cater to a specialized niche. Here are some to start with:

- ArticleCity.com (**www.articlecity.com**)
- EzineArticles.com (**www.ezinearticles.com**)
- GoArticles (**www.goarticles.com**)
- IdeaMarketers (**www.ideamarketers.com**)

Tip	To find more article directories, search for "free articles," "submit article," "free content," and "announcement lists" on your favorite search engine.

Article Marketing Services

For most people, submitting your articles manually to a few article sites is enough to generate a positive viral marketing response. But, if you want to submit multiple articles to multiple sites, you might want to consider outsourcing the task. Here are several services that offer article submission for a fee:

- Article Marketer (**www.articlemarketer.com**)

- Article Marketing Experts (**www.articlemarketingexperts.com**)
- iSnare (**www.isnare.com**)

Do-It-Yourself Article Marketing

Although the advantages are many, there are also some disadvantages to article marketing. For example, you can't control who publishes your articles. A site that you don't like or that is poorly designed may post your article.

If you're selective about who publishes your articles, you can try the do-it-yourself approach. Although this can be more time-consuming, it often generates more targeted results and helps you control whom you allow to republish your content. Using this approach, you should:

- Analyze the top websites and ezines that share your target audience yet don't compete directly with you. If you've done your homework, you already know which sites and ezines generate lots of traffic and have a large number of readers.
- Review your targets to determine whether articles by guest authors are appropriate. Even if they don't publish guest articles now, that doesn't mean they might not consider what you have to offer.
- Contact the sites and ezines directly, stating that you're an author with free reprint articles available. If the site regularly accepts such articles, submission directions may be posted. Otherwise, just contact the site owner or ezine editor.

▶ See chapter 6, "Promoting Your Book with an Ezine"

Posting Your Articles on Your Website

After creating your articles, post them on your website. Doing so offers several benefits:

- Search engines can find your articles and refer traffic to your website.
- The articles provide value-added content for site visitors who may not read your articles elsewhere.
- Visitors may like the articles they read on your site and request to reprint them. This is a good reason to include a note that free reprints are available on request.

Tip   Although they aren't really article marketing sites, converting your articles to content that works on high-traffic sites like Google Knol (**knol.google.com**), Squidoo (**www.squidoo.com**), and HubPages (**www.hubpages.com**) can also yield results.

Tracking Your Article Marketing Success

Tracking the success of your article marketing campaign is a critical step. In addition to reviewing your stats with any articles directories to which you submitted, set up alerts with Google Alerts (**www.google.com/alerts**) and Yahoo! Alerts (**alerts.yahoo.com**) using your exact article titles in quotations. Also review your web statistics for traffic coming from the sites hosting your articles. You'll soon see a pattern developing in terms of article placements, web traffic, and increased sales. Based on this information, adjust your article marketing campaign as needed.

Web-Savvy in Action

Amanda is a career coach and author of a book on making a successful career change. In order to attract more readers, as well as prospects for her online coaching services, she writes a series of five articles that she posts on several well-known article directories as well as on her own website.

Amanda creates a resource box that highlights her book, website, ezine, and coaching services with an offer of a free special report as an incentive to sign up for her ezine. In addition, her resource box provides a direct link to her website that includes her target keyword phrase "career changers" as anchor text to optimize search engine visibility.

Article Marketing Step-by-Step

A well-designed article marketing campaign that results in article placement on targeted, high-traffic sites can make a big difference in your web traffic and resulting sales. Here's what you need to do:

- ☐ Strategize on article ideas that would promote your book

- ☐ Write your articles following the format that works for article marketing

- ☐ Create a resource box that emphasizes your expertise and draws traffic to your site

- ☐ Post your articles on your own website or blog

- ☐ Submit your articles to article directories or through an article marketing service

- ☐ Consider direct submission to target websites if you want more control over the distribution of your articles

- ☐ Track your article marketing success using Google Alerts and Yahoo! Alerts as well as your own website statistics

13

Promoting Your Book with a Virtual Book Tour

A virtual book tour is similar to a traditional book tour except that the tour stops aren't at physical bookstores but at websites or blogs. The advantages of a virtual book tour are that it's less expensive than a traditional tour and offers the possibility of reaching far more people. In general, an in-person bookstore visit attracts only a modest crowd unless you're a well-known author. However, the results of a virtual tour remain available on most sites and blogs for a long time after the tour itself, making your information available to thousands of people who didn't participate at the actual time of your tour.

Virtual Book Tours 101

On a virtual book tour, you can:

- Act as a guest blogger on a blog
- Have a blogger discuss your book
- Participate in an online chat
- Participate in a text-based, audio, or podcast interview
- Answer questions from site visitors
- Offer prizes or freebies to site visitors
- Have your book reviewed
- Post original content or a book excerpt
- Create an online event

Ensuring a Successful Virtual Tour

Here are six key steps to ensuring a successful virtual tour.

Planning Ahead

You need some lead time to organize a virtual book tour that generates results. Although some bloggers can post new content in a matter of hours, other tour stops take time to arrange. The ideal time to start thinking about your tour is while you're still writing your book. Keep a file of any promotional ideas that relate to your upcoming tour.

Bookmark any interesting sites or blogs you'd like to visit on your tour as well as interesting articles about other virtual book tours. Then one to three months before your book is published, start making contact with your tour targets and create a tour schedule. Be careful, though, to schedule tour stops only after your book is available. Prepublication buzz can work for some books, but in general, you want potential readers to be able to buy your book immediately after hearing about it on your tour.

Use templates whenever possible to speed up the process of contacting sites, but be sure to customize them to show your tour target that you've done your research. If tour planning is too time-consuming, consider hiring a publicist experienced with virtual book tours or assigning the coordination effort to an assistant.

Selecting the Right Tour Stops

Choosing the right sites and blogs to visit on your virtual book tour is critical to its success. You probably already have some ideas about good candidates based on the sites that you visit now. To find others, you'll need to do some research.

When considering a potential tour stop, first verify that it serves your target market. Visiting a blog that has few readers who would be interested in your book isn't a good use of your time. The number of visitors a target "tour stop" draws is also an important consideration. The more people you reach during your tour, the greater your chances for success.

To determine how much traffic a site or blog receives, take a look at the statistics available at traffic monitors such as Metrics Market (**www.metricsmarket.com**) or TrafficEstimate (**www.trafficestimate.com**). Also, check out a site's Google PageRank using the Google Toolbar (**toolbar.google.com**).

Remember, though, that you're after quality and not just quantity. If you wrote a book about quilting, for example, a quilting blog with 5,000 monthly visitors could be a better target than a general crafting site with double the number of visitors.

Pacing Yourself

You can fit a virtual book tour into a compressed scheduled, such as a week or two, or you can extend your tour over several months. Some authors even like to create a catchy tagline that describes their tour such as "30 blogs in 30 days," "around the web in 90 days," or "10 countries in 10 days." Whatever schedule you choose, be sure that you pace yourself. Do you have other commitments during this timeframe or is book promotion your sole emphasis? Even though you don't have to leave home, remember that tours requiring online chats, phone interviews, teleseminars, and other live events can be tiring.

Involving Your Publicist

If your publisher has assigned a publicist to promote your book or you hired your own publicist to help with your promotion efforts, be sure to involve this person in your virtual book tour. Even if you schedule your own tour stops, an experienced publicist can offer solid advice and ideas that you hadn't considered. Creating a solid partnership with available publicity resources can only improve the success of your tour.

Being Unique

Virtual book tours are still new enough to generate interest, but that doesn't mean you shouldn't make an extra effort to come up with a unique angle for your tour.

Be creative. Don't just give away a book; consider offering a big ticket item such as a free coaching session to entice potential readers on a high traffic site. Make a special offer to encourage visits to your own website, where visitors can sign up for your ezine and learn more about your book. Focus interviews and chats around topics that will generate buzz rather than simply focusing on you and your book.

By making each tour stop an event, you'll draw a larger audience and generate more publicity and more profits.

Publicizing Your "Tour" Everywhere

Again, the relative newness of a virtual book tour can make it easier to get publicity for your own tour, but you still need to get the word out. Here are several ideas that work well:

- Prominently feature your tour on your website, blog, and ezine to generate buzz and excitement—and for ongoing, 24/7 promotion.
- Seek out promotional opportunities with any writing, publishing, or professional organizations to which you belong. Organization websites, blogs, and newsletters are usually happy to mention member news and promotional activities.
- Ask your tour stop websites and blogs to promote their participation in your tour.
- Publish a press release, optimized with keywords and links, through an online press distribution service to reach both the media and your target audience.
- Continue publicity after the tour by posting tour results on your own sites.

▶ See chapter 11, "Promoting Your Book with Online Press Releases"

A virtual book tour can generate buzz and book sales that extend far beyond the actual timeframe of your tour. Focus on your target audience, generate pre-and post-tour publicity, and then reap the rewards of your tour for months, or even years, to come.

Finding Virtual Book Tour Stops That Generate Results

Finding the right stops for your tour is one of the most important things you can do to ensure its success. To start, you probably already have several stops in mind based on the sites and blogs you visit currently. After that, you need to do some research. First, think carefully about the target audience you want to reach and then formulate keywords that relate to this audience and your book's topic. From there, search for good prospects on:

- Major search engines (Google, Yahoo!, and Microsoft Live Search)
- Tagging and social bookmarking sites (Technorati, del.icio.us, and StumbleUpon)
- Blog directories (Google Blog Search and BlogCatalog)
- Podcast directories (Yahoo! Podcasts and iTunes)

Depending on the topic of your book, consider sites and blogs that focus on:

- Writing and books, particularly related to your genre
- The setting of your book
- Another aspect of your book (for example, if your novel is about a chef, you could also target food-related sites)
- Women's issues, if you're a female author
- Working at home, if you're a full-time at-home writer

Although searching online is one of the best ways to find stops on a virtual tour, it isn't the only way. Here are four more tips for finding great tour stops:

- Talk with other authors and people you know about the sites they visit.
- Look offline for potential tour targets. Read magazines and newspapers for ideas.
- Don't be afraid to include a stop that doesn't meet the initial requirement of reaching your specific audience or generating enough traffic. A little variety can enliven any tour.
- Go global. With English-language sites in Canada, the U.K., Australia, New Zealand, and many other countries, look outside the U.S. for potential tour stops.

Web-Savvy in Action

Nicole is a pastry chef and author of a book on low-fat, low-fuss desserts. To promote her new book, she conducted a virtual book tour. Over the course of a week, Nicole:

- Received four book reviews on high-traffic websites
- Offered a free recipe booklet to visitors of a well-known women's website for signing up for her ezine that week
- Served as a guest blogger on two cooking-related blogs
- Was interviewed on two podcasts
- Participated in an online chat on a home and garden website
- Published excerpts of her book on three websites
- Was interviewed for an audio segment on a cooking website in Australia

Virtual Book Tours Step-by-Step

A virtual book tour enables you to reach thousands more potential readers than any in-person tour. Here's how to do it:

- ☐ Strategize the goals of your tour and plan each "tour stop" in advance
- ☐ Select tour stops that focus on your target audience or a related audience, emphasizing high-traffic sites
- ☐ Add some global tour stops for impact and expanded sales opportunities
- ☐ Involve your publisher's publicist if one has been assigned
- ☐ Do something unique on your tour that will generate buzz
- ☐ Publicize your tour everywhere—on your website, blog, and podcast
- ☐ Ask for cooperative publicity from your tour stops
- ☐ Submit a press release to announce your tour
- ☐ Continue publicity after the tour by posting tour results on your website

14

Promoting Your Book
Through Social Networking

Social networking is currently a hot topic and its popularity is predicted to grow even more over the next decade. Social bookmarking extends the "social" aspect of information-sharing across the web. Integrating social networking into your online book promotion plan is a smart, strategic move and, fortunately, one that's easy to implement.

Quick Fact	Social networking sites will grow 47 percent, year over year, reaching 45 percent of web users (a total of 68.8 million). —*Source: Nielsen//NetRatings*

Social Networking 101

Social networking sites are websites designed to connect you with likeminded people. These web-based communities include features such as profiles, chats, forums, blogs, video, and more for members to communicate with each other. Essentially, it's traditional personal networking moved to the web, where your potential contacts are all over the world, not just in your city.

Quick Fact	Because of the enormous traffic surge, advertising on social networking sites has become a top priority. By 2010, spending will hit $2.15 billion to reach this huge market. —*eMarketer*

Generating Social Networking Buzz

Joining and participating on social networking sites offers numerous advantages. You can:

- Connect with other authors, many of whom are potential readers of your book
- Connect with current and future readers
- Get links back to your website

Keep in mind that to benefit from social networking you need to participate. Signing up and never returning to a site has little effect. You need to join the right sites and become an active participant, at least on a weekly basis.

To avoid becoming overwhelmed with all the options, do some research before joining. Start with a few of the best options, such as an author site, a specialty site, and a general interest site. Begin participation and grow from there. Some authors love networking and join multiple sites. Others prefer to focus on just a few. If you don't see a benefit after a few weeks, consider trying another site.

Tip	To see how many web visits you're receiving from a particular social networking site, check your web statistics. This can tell you quickly how well your investment in time is paying off.

Social Networking Sites for Authors

The number of social networking sites for authors has grown tremendously over the past few years.

Here are a few sites to try:

- AuthorNation (**www.authornation.com**)
- AuthorsDen (**www.authorsden.com**)
- Book Marketing Network (**bookmarket.ning.com**)
- GoodReads (**www.goodreads.com**)
- LibraryThing (**www.librarything.com**)
- Shelfari (**www.shelfari.com**)

MySpace

With site visitors reaching 100 million per month, MySpace (**www.myspace.com**) is one of the most popular social networking sites around as well as one of the most visited sites on the web. Although MySpace can be a great book promotion tool, it isn't for every author.

| **Quick Fact** | The top search term for all of 2006 was "MySpace." *—Hitwise* |

MySpace can be beneficial to authors of:

- Fiction and nonfiction aimed at young adults
- Category fiction such as romance, science fiction, and fantasy
- Nonfiction books aimed at a general audience

Authors of literary fiction, academic books, or business-related titles don't tend to do as well with the MySpace community.

| **Quick Fact** | Sixty-eight percent of the MySpace user base is over 25 years old. MySpace's largest audience segment is between 35 and 54, comprising 40 percent of total users. *—ComScore Networks* |

If you want to give MySpace a try, sign up and create a free profile. The default settings may not give you the look you desire, so consider doing a little customization.

To promote your book on MySpace, you'll want to take care of the obvious tasks first, such as posting information about your book and links to your website or blog. In addition, here are some more ways to maximize your MySpace exposure:

- Focus on friendships. Make friends with as many other authors and potential readers as possible. Soon their friends may become your friends as well.
- Post a calendar of your upcoming book events.
- Add a subscription box to your ezine.
- Post excerpts or links to excerpts. People like to try before they buy.
- Become a groupie. By joining MySpace groups, you expand your reach even further. Look for groups that focus on authors, writing, and the topic of your books.
- Minimize overt sales pitches; focus on quality content.
- Learn about all of MySpace's features (blogs, bulletins, and so forth) and start using the ones that you think will work for you.

To view a sample author MySpace profile, visit **www.myspace.com/websavvywriter**.

| **Tip** | Just like a website, the information you post on social networking sites is public. For your own safety, be wary of posting your home address, phone number, and so forth. In general, a little common sense should help you avoid any potential pitfalls and focus on the benefits of social networking. |

Facebook

With more than 100 million active users, Facebook (**www.facebook.com**) is another "must" for authors seeking social networking exposure.

To get started on Facebook, you need to create a profile. Facebook profiles include typical information about your background, interests, and work. But you can also enliven your Facebook profile with additional content in the form of Facebook applications. Some relevant applications for authors include:

- Photos (show off your book covers or photos from author signings or events)
- Web Presence (links to your websites)
- My Box (great for adding more details about your books)
- Business Cards
- MyLinkedIn Profile
- Twitter
- Blog RSS Feed Reader

With new applications launching all the time, you're sure to find some of your own favorites as well. To view a sample profile with all of the above applications, befriend me on Facebook at **www.facebook.com/people/Patrice-Anne_Rutledge/731634112**.

In addition to setting up a profile, also consider creating a Facebook page for your book or business and a Facebook group to encourage discussion on your book's topic. If you host events, Facebook Events can help you spread the word.

The Best of the Rest—Other Social Networking Sites to Consider

Here's a selected list of other social networking sites worth exploring. Some are for a general audience and others focus on a specific area such as business networking.

- Bebo (**www.bebo.com**)
- BlackPlanet (**www.blackplanet.com**)
- CafeMom (**www.cafemom.com**)
- Ecademy (**www.ecademy.com**)
- LinkedIn (**www.linkedin.com**)
- Ryze (**www.ryze.com**)
- Twitter (**www.twitter.com**)
- Viadeo (**www.viadeo.com**)
- XING (**www.xing.com**)

If you join Ryze or Ecademy, check out Ecademy Writers and Publishers and Ryze Writers & Editors (**writerseditors-network.ryze.com**).

Web-Savvy in Action	Colette is the author of several romance novels who also is a writing instructor. To expand her online network and increase visibility of her books, she joins several social networks: an author network, Facebook, and a general interest site. She creates a detailed profile on all three with links to her book trailers, excerpts, and teaching schedule and begins to participate. Very quickly, Colette notices an increase in her site traffic and soon, an increase in her sales and class sign-ups as well.

As an active social networker, I participate on several sites including Facebook, LinkedIn, Book Marketing Network, MySpace, Ecademy, Twitter, Viadeo, and XING. Please feel free to connect with me if you join as well.

Want even more social networking? Check out Wikipedia's detailed list of social networking sites: **en.wikipedia.org/wiki/List_of_social_networking_websites**.

Promoting Your Book Through Social Bookmarking

Another related option is promoting your book through social bookmarking websites such as Digg (**www.digg.com**), del.icio.us (**del.icio.us**), reddit (**www.reddit.com**), and StumbleUpon (**www.stumbleupon.com**). These sites offer a way to share your favorite bookmarks (links to websites, blogs, and so forth) with others, including links to your own articles and blog posts. Be careful to bookmark only useful, relevant content. This isn't the time for a heavy self-promotional approach.

Including social bookmarking buttons next to your content encourages others to bookmark it as well. See my blog (**www.websavvywriter.com**) for an example of how to make it easy for readers to bookmark blog posts. I used the WordPress ShareThis (**www.sharethis.com**) plug-in to do this.

Social Networking Step-by-Step

Social networking can quickly and easily connect you with readers around the world. Here's how to get started:

- ☐ Research social networking to understand how it works and determine which sites are the best match for you and your audience

- ☐ Sign up with no more than three social networking sites to start

- ☐ Create a detailed profile that encourages people to check out your book

- ☐ Follow the often unwritten "rules" of each site on which you participate; some allow more self-promotion than others

- ☐ Participate regularly on your selected social networks

- ☐ Review your website statistics to determine how much traffic you're receiving from your selected sites

- ☐ If time permits or you aren't generating results from your selected sites, begin active participation on other sites

- ☐ Create simple profiles on the sites on which you don't anticipate participation, for the sake of basic visibility

- ☐ Bookmark your most useful, interesting content on social bookmarking sites such as Digg, del.icio.us, reddit, and StumbleUpon

- ☐ Enable your site and blog visitors to easily bookmark your content

15

Twelve More Ways to Promote Your Book Online

In addition to creating a website, blog, ezine, or podcast, other online marketing techniques can also generate interest in your book. Some take only a few minutes to implement.

Quick Fact	The number of consumers who tune out traditional media and advertising, and use consumer-to-consumer communication like blogging, mobile messaging, comparison shopping sites, word-of-mouth marketing, and peer-to-peer networks continues to rise. —*Source: Devices & Access Online Survey, Forrester Research, Inc., 2005*

Get Listed in Directories

The web is filled with directories, including sites offering profiles of their members, services matching up independent professionals with customers, and much more.

Writers' Association Websites

Many writing websites, including those sponsored by writers' associations, provide an online listing of their members. If you belong to any writers' associations, check out their website to see if they offer member listings.

Some sites that offer member listings include:

- American Society of Journalists and Authors (**www.asja.org**)
- Australian Society of Authors (**www.asauthors.org**)
- Authors Guild (**www.authorsguild.org**)
- Canadian Authors Association (**www.canauthors.org**)
- mediabistro.com (**www.mediabistro.com**)

- Media Kitty (**www.mediakitty.com**)
- Mystery Writers of America (**www.mysterywriters.org**)
- National Association of Science Writers (**www.nasw.org**)
- New Zealand Society of Authors (**www.authors.org.nz**)
- Romance Writers of America (**www.rwanational.org**)
- Science Fiction and Fantasy Writers of America (**www.sfwa.org**)
- Society of Authors (**www.societyofauthors.net**)

Niche Directories

Whatever your area of expertise, there's most likely one or more online directories on that topic. You're probably already aware of several directories in your field. To find more, do a web search on relevant keywords.

Expert Listings

If you're a specialist in your field, get listed as an expert so that journalists can contact you for potential interviews. Two excellent sources include:

- **Business Wire ExpertSource** (**www.businesswire.com**). Business Wire sponsors the ExpertSource expert database. You can enter a profile in the ExpertSource database if you're a Business Wire member.
- **ProfNet** (**profnet.prnewswire.com**). PR Newswire sponsors the fee-based Prof-Net expert database.

To review the existing expert profiles in ProfNet and ExpertSource, sign up for a free media account. As an author, you most likely qualify. Both of these databases are also great resources if you're looking for an expert to interview for one of your own writing projects.

Web-Savvy in Action

Oliver is a happiness coach who is the author of a book on finding happiness in a stressful world. To publicize his book and his speaking and coaching services, Oliver hopes to achieve major media coverage.

He decides that listing himself as an expert should help achieve his goals, so he secures listings in the two most prominent expert databases. Oliver creates a media-friendly profile and ensures the online media kit on his website is current and intriguing.

In addition, he joins several popular media leads services that forward potential leads to him directly.

Google Local

If you have a business related to your book, consider adding yourself to Google Local (**www.google.com/local/add**), Google's searchable database for people seeking nearby businesses. Best of all, a listing is free.

Participate in Google Book Search

Google Book Search (**books.google.com**) enables users to search the full text of participating books and preview selected content. Links to purchase the book from retailers such as Amazon.com and Barnes & Noble appear next to the book's table of contents and page views. Google Book Search is a free, voluntary program that helps generate visibility and additional sales for participating books.

You're eligible to sign up for Google Book Search if you self-published or currently have the rights to your book. Otherwise, your publisher must initiate participation. By searching on your name or your book title, you may discover that your book is already included in the program. When I searched for my name, I found several recent books already listed.

Tip	Microsoft used to offer a similar program, the Live Search Books Publisher Program, but discontinued it in May 2008.

Participate on Online Chats

Online chats aren't as popular as they once were, but they can still be viable online book promotion tools. The website hosting your chat normally publicizes it, which can generate additional buzz even if you don't attract a large audience.

Create a Squidoo Lens

Squidoo (**www.squidoo.com**) enables you to create "lenses" about any particular topic of interest to share your information and ideas with likeminded people. You can promote your book, add blog posts, or link to affiliate sites from your lens—giving you the opportunity to both publicize and profit. To see an example of a Squidoo lens, see my Online Book Promotion lens at **www.squidoo.com/book_promotion**.

Use Autoresponders for Promotion and Profits

An autoresponder is a program that sends automatic replies to anyone who sends an email to a specific email address. For example, let's say that you want to offer a free ecourse delivered over seven days. You could announce this course on your website and direct site visitors to send an email to freecourse@yourwebsite.com to sign up.

The autoresponder would then send a thank-you email and the first lesson to anyone who signed up, delivering the next six lessons over the course of a week. Other than creating the content for each day of the course and setting up the autoresponder, you don't need to do anything. Everyone who requests this course gets a response almost immediately. It doesn't matter if you're away from your computer, asleep, or on a beach in Tahiti.

You can use autoresponders to automatically:

- Provide more information to anyone who sends an email to a specific email address
- Deliver an ecourse on a specified schedule
- Send an email to site visitors who fill out a form or take a specific action
- Deliver an automated response to any email

Many web hosts offer basic autoresponders, however, you should consider full-service autoresponder functionality to get access to advanced features and track your autoresponder success. Several companies offer autoresponders in addition to ecommerce and email marketing services. Some to consider include:

- 1ShoppingCart.com (**www.1shoppingcart.com**)
- AWeber (**www.aweber.com**)
- iContact (**www.icontact.com**)

▸ See chapter 7, "Selling and Promoting Your Book with Ecommerce," Full-Service Shopping Cart Solutions

Teach Online

Teaching online is another good way to promote your book while generating income. In addition to being qualified to teach writing classes, you can also teach on your area of expertise. Many organizations offer online training opportunities including professional associations, elearning websites, colleges, and universities.

Quick Fact

Thirteen percent of American Internet users, or nearly 19 million people, have taken a class online for personal enjoyment or enrichment.
—*Source: Pew Internet & American Life Project*

Some online training websites to look into include:

- **ed2go** (**www.ed2go.com**). Offers over 300 courses delivered online through more than 1,200 colleges in the United States, Canada, and Australia.
- **Podclass.com** (**www.podclass.com**). Create both free and fee online classes using their streamlined learning environment.
- **WorldWideLearn** (**www.worldwidelearn.com**). A comprehensive elearning directory that lists online courses in nearly 400 subject areas.
- **Writers.com** (**www.writers.com**). Offers classes for fiction and nonfiction writers.

In general, your qualifications are more important than actual teaching credentials for most online teaching opportunities. However, it's still important to have a basic foundation in adult learning principles and the common practices of online learning … or at least be willing to develop this knowledge.

Tip

Think of your instructor bio for an online class as an additional form of free publicity. Be sure to mention the titles of your books as well as your website URL in any instructor bio.

In addition to teaching online classes for other organizations, also consider developing your own online classes, creating free ecourses available by autoresponder, or delivering fee-based or free teleseminars.

Web-Savvy in Action

Skye is a feng shui consultant and author of a book on her specialty. As a former teacher, she would like to use teaching as a way to publicize her book. She is already teaching seminars and workshops in her local area, but she wants to expand her reach by teaching online. She contacts several companies that offer online courses and arranges to teach a four-week feng shui course through a well-known online learning site.

She also develops a more personalized online course that she offers independently on her own website. Over the next few weeks, she plans to convert the course to a downloadable MP3. Finally, to introduce potential customers to the basic concepts of feng shui, Skye offers a free autoresponder ecourse that she promotes on her website and in articles she writes for her ezine and other sites.

Create a Strong Signature Files

Email programs enable you to include a signature file with contact information at the end of the messages you send. If you choose your words carefully on these few lines of text, they can help you promote your book and your business. If you specialize in more than one area, you can create multiple signature files and choose which is most appropriate in any given situation. For example, I've created the following signature files:

#1: Long, General Signature File

Patrice-Anne Rutledge
Bestselling Author (26 books translated into 11 languages)
Book Publishing & Promotion Expert
CeM-certified Social Media Strategist
http://www.patricerutledge.com
http://www.websavvywriter.com
patrice@patricerutledge.com

Recent Titles:
The Web-Savvy Writer: Book Promotion with a High-Tech Twist (Pacific Ridge Press)
The Truth About Profiting from Social Networking (Pearson/FT Press)
Special Edition Using Microsoft Office PowerPoint 2007 (Pearson/Que)

#2: Short, General Signature File

Patrice-Anne Rutledge
Bestselling Author
Book Publishing & Promotion Expert
CeM-certified Social Media Strategist
http://www.patricerutledge.com
patrice@patricerutledge.com

#3: Short, Book Publishing & Promotion Signature File

Patrice-Anne Rutledge
Bestselling Author (26 books translated into 11 languages)
Book Publishing & Promotion Expert
Author, The Web-Savvy Writer: Book Promotion with a High-Tech Twist
http://www.websavvywriter.com
patrice@websavvywriter.com

Participate on Online Book Review and Author Sites

Listing yourself with a website link on as many quality sites as possible provides enhanced web visibility, improves your search engine ranking, and generates more traffic. Here are some book and author sites to consider:

- **Author Reviews (www.author-reviews.com).** Posts free book synopses as well as excerpts from reviews you've received.
- **AuthorsandExperts.com (www.authorsandexperts.com).** Fee-based membership includes a searchable directory listing and access to media want ads.
- **AuthorsOnTheWeb.com (www.authorsontheweb.com).** Publishes author bibliographies as well as lists of soon-to-be-published books.
- **AuthorYellowPages.com (www.authoryellowpages.com).** Offers author listings for a fee.
- **Bookreporter.com (www.bookreporter.com).** Publishes reviews, author interviews, author profiles, and other features. The focus is on fiction and narrative nonfiction.
- **FaithfulReader.com (www.faithfulreader.com).** A Christian book site offering author interviews and profiles, study guides, and book features.
- **Kidsreads.com (www.kidsreads.com).** Offers reviews for children ages 6 to 12.
- **ReadingGroupGuides.com (www.readinggroupguides.com).** Offers reading group guides for fiction and nonfiction titles, most submitted by publishers.
- **Teenreads.com (www.teenreads.com).** Publishes book reviews, author profiles, and a monthly newsletter focusing on books targeting a teen audience.

Tip

Many other websites review books. Some sites focus specifically on books; others include reviews as well as additional content. To find more potential book review targets, do a web search on "book review," or narrow your search to the type of book you write such as "cookbook review."

Create Supplemental Information Products

Many authors, particularly nonfiction authors, make more money selling other products and services than they do from their actual books. In addition to speaking and consulting, here's a list of other items you can sell online that both promote your book and generate revenue:

- Downloadable audio seminars and audio CDs
- Teleseminars, teleseminar CDs, and teleseminar transcripts
- Ebooks and special reports
- DVDs, videos, and online video tutorials

- Email and telephone coaching
- Online courses, both interactive and autoresponder
- Subscriptions to members-only website content
- Bundled collections and kits
- Branded items related to your book, such as calendars, journals, and clothing

---

Web-Savvy in Action

Beau is the author of a book on podcasting. It's selling well, but he'd like to increase his income and create some content on new technologies that were still emerging at the time he wrote his book. Beau decides to create a CD training course on video podcasting, providing both a step-by-step instruction guide as well as several tutorial screencasts.

In addition to selling his training CD from his website, Beau lists it on Amazon.com through its CreateSpace program, on popular auction sites such as eBay, as well as on Froogle, the free shopping search engine. The added exposure on these popular sites both increases sales as well as drives more traffic to his website.

▶ See chapter 7, "Selling and Promoting Your Book with Ecommerce"

▶ See chapter 8, "Selling and Promoting Your Book on Amazon.com," Amazon Advantage

▶ See chapter 10, "Promoting Your Book with Audio and Video"

Create Your Own Affiliate Program

In addition to generating affiliate commissions by recommending other products to your audience, you can also increase sales by offering affiliate commissions to people who recommend *your* products to their own audience.

Creating your own affiliate program works best for authors who produce supplemental products such as ebooks, special reports, audio, and so forth. If this is something you're interested in, look for an ecommerce solution that includes the option of setting up an affiliate program. Some good choices include:

- 1ShoppingCart.com (**www.1shoppingcart.com**)
- ClickBank (**www.clickbank.com**)
- PayLoadz (**www.payloadz.com**)

▶ See chapter 7, "Promoting Your Book with Ecommerce," Selling Books from Your Website

▶ See chapter 9, "Promoting Your Book with Online Advertising," Affiliate Marketing Revenue

Participate on Message Boards, Newsgroups, and Lists

Every topic has at least several message boards, newsgroups, and mailing lists where like-minded people discuss shared interests. Your participation can help position yourself as an expert in the eyes of the other participants and serve as a promotional tool for your books.

Tip	To find groups and mailing lists, check out Google Groups (**groups.google.com**) and Yahoo! Groups (**groups.yahoo.com**).

Because keeping up with multiple boards can be time-consuming, be selective about the ones on which you want to participate. Your focus should be on boards that are frequented by a large number of people in your target audience. A board with participants who post intelligent messages under their own names is usually a good sign. Avoid posting messages that are overt advertisements for your book, website, or other services. Instead, offer helpful advice or commentary without sales hype. Let your signature file do the promotion for you.

Web-Savvy in Action	Monique is the author of a parenting book focused on raising responsible teens. She wants to develop an extensive online book promotion campaign, but she has a small budget. After conducting some preliminary research, Monique coordinates a no-cost promotional campaign in which she plans to:

- Request listings in the online member directories of the writers' associations to which she belongs
- Create a signature file that includes her website URL and the name of her book
- Distribute monthly press releases on parenting issues and submit them to free press release distribution services (while budgeting for more comprehensive distribution in the future)
- Write a series of parenting articles and submit them to article directories
- Participate in online chats and on message boards hosted by high-traffic parenting sites
- Create a profile on author and book sites that offer free listings

Online Marketing Step-by-Step

After you've covered the basics, there are still many other online book promotion opportunities for you to consider. Here's your "to do" list of other ideas to explore:

- ☐ List yourself in all appropriate directories, including writers' association directories, niche directories, expert listings, and even Google Local

- ☐ Create book excerpts to interest potential readers, ideally in PDF format

- ☐ Sign up for Google Book Search or request your publisher to do so

- ☐ Join or host an online chat on your book's topic

- ☐ Create an autoresponder, such as an ecourse, to generate interest in your book

- ☐ Teach an online course related to your book, either through an existing program or university or on your own

- ☐ Design one or more signature files to sell your books with every email you send

- ☐ Submit your book to online book review sites, or ask your publisher's publicist to do so

- ☐ Explore publicity opportunities with all websites that offer author listings, interviews, and excerpts

- ☐ Create supplemental products such as special reports, audio downloads, and CDs that complement your book and increase your revenue

- ☐ Create and implement your own affiliate program for others to promote your books and products

- ☐ Participate in appropriate message boards, newsgroups, and mailing lists that reach your target audience

Appendix: Author Profiles

In this appendix, you'll read about twelve authors who have mastered the art of online book promotion. Some are using the latest technologies such as podcasting and video; others are following a more conventional path to online book promotion. Whatever approach they're taking, they have found a unique way to profit from their web presence.

In alphabetical order, these authors are:

- Peter Bowerman
- Ann Douglas
- Tom Evslin
- Lee Foster
- Diana L. Guerrero
- Shirley Jump
- Tee Morris
- Angie Pedersen
- Paris Permenter and John Bigley
- Dan Poynter
- Stephanie Roberts

Author Profile: Peter Bowerman

www.wellfedwriter.com

Peter Bowerman is the author of the 2000 Book-of-the-Month Club selection, *The Well-Fed Writer* and its 2005 companion volume, *TWFW: Back For Seconds* (both self-published), how-to "standards" on writing for businesses, large and small, and for rates of $50 to more than $125 an hour. In 2006, he released *The Well-Fed Self-Publisher: How to Turn One Book into a Full-Time Living*.

How much time do you spend on online book promotion as compared to traditional book marketing?

My approach is almost exclusively online-based. Because my books are niche books (about the field of lucrative commercial freelancing), pursuing mainstream media attention is usually futile. As a rule, they don't care about a book and subject like mine. The only exception is when I'm actually going to a city to do an event, conference, seminar, book signing, and so forth. In those cases, I'll contact the media as I'm incrementally more newsworthy since I'm going to actually be there.

How important are your website and ezine in developing your brand and an audience for your books?

(laughs) A better question would be, "How could any author who's even remotely serious about promoting his or her work *not* have a website?" A website is absolutely non-negotiable—it's the linchpin of any marketing campaign—it's where all roads lead. As for an ezine, obviously not as essential, but mine has been crucial in building a community amongst my readership. It's the one thing I do monthly that touches all my readers (and prospective readers), and keeps them close. For those who haven't bought my books yet, an ezine is a great baby step for them to "test-drive" me and my offering. Eventually, a lot of those folks become buyers.

What online promotion techniques do you find most effective for attracting media attention? What has been your experience with distributing online press releases and creating an online media kit on your website?

Again, I haven't tried very hard to attract mainstream media attention, given the niche nature of my work. I've had FAR better success identifying my target audiences (writers, at-home moms, home-based business seekers, the 55+ crowd, and so forth), going to where they hang out on the Internet (there are zillions of sites catering to all the above crowds), and contacting the founder/owner to see if I can get a review copy into their hands, write an article for their site, have them do a Q&A with me, post a blurb on the site, or any combination of the above.

The "Media Resources Section" of my site (**www.wellfedwriter.com/media.shtml**, closest thing to an online media kit), I think, is essential to have for ANY potential reviewer, wherever they come from. It's all about making it easy for someone to give you some exposure. If someone has to hunt to find what they need (author pictures, cover art, blurbs, bio, press release, sample chapters, and so forth), they might just not bother.

What's your opinion on ebooks as a supplemental revenue stream for print books?

As an adjunct to a hard copy version, they're a total no-brainer. No production costs (just get your hard-copy book's typesetter to slap your cover artwork onto the front of the finished file, turn the whole thing into a PDF, and you're done). No warehousing, inventory, or shipping costs—it's pure profit. And they'll help you sell hard copy books. I know a lot of my ebook buyers (because of the nature of my book) get part way through my books, and say, "the heck with it; I want the real book so I can make notes and mark it up."

What online book promotion tool, that you aren't currently using, are you most interested in trying and why?

I'd like to explore Google AdWords ads. I think it might just be a good fit for my topics, and it's cheap enough and low-risk enough that there's no reason not to give it a shot (except finding the time in the day to explore one more item on my massive to-do list…). I get a decent number of folks who tell me they stumbled across my site and I'd like to try to catch more of those surfers in my net…

Author Profile: Ann Douglas

anndouglas.blogspot.com

Ann Douglas is the author of 28 books including the bestselling The Mother of All Books series with titles such as *The Mother of All Pregnancy Books* and *The Mother of All Baby Books*. She is currently in the process of launching a spin-off series with her publisher, Wiley—The Mother of All Solutions series. The first two titles will be *Sleep Solutions for Your Baby, Toddler, and Preschooler* and *Mealtime Solutions for Your Baby, Toddler, and Preschooler*. Read Ann's lengthier bio at **www.pregnancylibrary.com/meetanndouglas.html**.

How much time do you spend on online book promotion as compared to traditional book marketing?

The majority of my book promotion is done online. I am away touring one to two weeks per year, I do about five media interviews per week by phone from my office, and I make a couple of TV appearances per month by traveling to nearby cities. All my other book promotion is done online. I probably spend one to two hours per day on online promotion.

I have a number of websites (**www.having-a-baby.com**, **www. parentinglibrary.com**, **www.pregnancylibrary.com**, and **www.canuckchicks.com**). I'm in the process of developing **www.motherofallsolutions.com** right now.

How do you use Amazon.com as a book promotion tool?

I participate in the AmazonConnect program so that I can stay in touch with people who have purchased my books or who have indicated that they'd like to receive posts from my blog in their "plog" (Amazon's term for the Amazon customer's message area for author posts). I also use the site's tagging feature (to create genuinely useful lists for site visitors). I create So You'd Like to … guides and Listmania! lists that are designed to provide readers with useful information. And, I will occasionally post mini-reviews of books that I have particularly enjoyed. Amazon can be addictive, so I really have to limit my time at the site.

What I'm trying to do increasingly is create online content in my own blog or website and then throw to that from my AmazonConnect author blog. That way, I don't have to give Amazon a license to the content (something that automatically happens when you create anything on the site); nor do I have to stick to using Amazon's content creation tools. I can use color, fun fonts, etc. in the world beyond Amazon.com such as my downloadable tipsheets at **www.parentinglibrary.com**. And because I'm linking to Amazon.com (and linking back from my own site), this is good from a search engine optimization perspective.

You host several other websites including PregnancyLibrary.com and ParentingLibrary.com. What impact has the success of these sites had on the marketing of your books?

Some sites that are reluctant to link to sites that are clearly book promotion-oriented don't have a problem with linking to a web guide-type site. So having different types of sites and blogs makes me more linkable. Blogs like to link to blogs; non-commercial sites like to link to non-commercial sites. If I can be different types of things to different types of online entities, it's easier to form web partnerships. Also—these URLs are easier to give out during radio interviews than having-a-baby.com. That's an important consideration when registering a domain name.

How do you use your blog to convey a sense of personality and connect with your audience?

I've always done a lot of online web chats as part of my book promotion activities (web chats at sites like BabyCenter.com and online courses at sites like WebMD.com). I've been told over the years that my personality is a natural for the web. I tend to be really friendly and outgoing—and a bit wacky. So I carry that personality over to my blog.

I have a loyal group of readers who link to and read my blog and I, in turn, read a fair number of their blogs, too. The "momosphere" is a warm and friendly place to be, both as an author and a mom. I interview a lot of pregnancy/parenting authors in my blog because this helps to bring more readers to my blog and supports the work of other people who are doing good work in the parenting field (Mom University and Author University features).

Blogging has actually been far more beneficial to me as a writer than I had anticipated when I first launched my blog. It has encouraged me to write in a really fun, free-flowing style and to take creative risks with my writing. That has improved the overall quality of my writing, both on and off the blog. I even signed up for a fiction-writing course last fall because I was eager to experiment with short story writing, all as a direct result of my blog. So while I launched it with the intention of using it as a book promotion tool, it has become so much more than that for me. It's become a creative outlet, a professional development tool, and a way to connect with other writers and parents. Anyone who pooh-poohs blogging simply doesn't understand the power of blogging.

What online book promotion tool, that you aren't currently using, are you most interested in trying and why?

I'm interested in getting involved in podcasting, but I've been so busy writing books in the past year that I haven't had the time to tackle that. But I hope to do that during the next year. I'd also like to use more bells and whistles on my websites (reader surveys and video and audio clips). Once again, all that's stopping me is the need to cap the amount of time I spend on promotion. I find marketing and promotion really fun and creative, but it can become all-encompassing and take you away from your writing work, if you're not careful. Sometimes I find that I have to close all my browser windows and turn off my email in order to get any work done. There's always some cool online promotion activity I could be engaged in, if only I had a few more minutes....

Author Profile: Tom Evslin

www.hackoff.com
blog.tomevslin.com

Tom Evslin—recently retired from a career as a serial high-tech entrepreneur, including several startups, an IPO, and stints at AT&T and Microsoft—writes about what he knows. hackoff.com is his first novel and is an historic murder mystery set in the Internet bubble and rubble. Fractals of Change (**blog.tomevslin.com**, which is pretty widely read) is nonfiction based on a lifetime of experience in the high-tech business.

Why did you decide to create hackoff.com as a blook?

Debut authors know they will have to do their own marketing and publicity. I already had a blog with a number of readers and hoped that other bloggers would provide word-of-blog to make up for the mainstream reviews I knew would be hard to get. They've done that very generously.

Distributing the online edition as a blook let me create buzz with no cost of distribution, which has already led to presales of the hardcover edition on Amazon.com and 800ceoread. Technology like RSS, with a little tinkering, was ideal for serialization and subscription.

An online book (blook) can have things the hardcover won't, like live links and the faux company website we set up. Online readers have been very much like beta testers and helped me find bugs in both text and plot.

It made special sense to me to start online since the book takes place in the first Internet bubble and since so much of my career has been online. The technology and speed of execution of the web are much more familiar and comfortable to me than the technologies and slow pace of offline book publishing. Being online let us create a market for the book during the time it takes a hardcover to get produced and printed.

But many people—even those who've sampled hackoff.com online—still want a book they can hold in their hands and take to the beach. The paper edition—in our case hardcover first—is still a necessary choice.

You offer a variety of ways to access your blook—as text-based blog entries, in PDF format, as an audio podcast, via email, via RSS, and in print. What is the benefit in doing this? What format has proved the most popular?

The web is all about choice. Different people prefer to access their entertainment in different ways. So each edition broadens the number of people reading and listening to the story.

RSS serialization of text has been the most popular so far but podcast serialization started recently and is growing very fast. Note that either text or audio can be accessed online or through text or email serialization and the podcast is also available through Podiobooks.com and iTunes. The email option is getting a steadily higher share of serialization as our audience, which initially started as almost all blog readers, expands to those who don't know what RSS and feed readers are.

How will your blook tour help you further connect with your target audience?

We're just about to start out on the blook tour so I can't give you the results yet. Details are available on our publisher's website: **www.dothillpress.com**.

Basically, we think this is a way to band together with the authors of other blooks to promote and cross-promote. Bloggers like getting the guest content. We authors like the exposure.

What online promotion techniques do you find most effective for attracting media attention?

Most of our media push so far has been towards the technical press, both because I know people there and because it's relatively easy to get their attention for the technologies we've been using and tweaking. There is some interest in the financial press based on content—there's lots of curiosity about what the bubble looked like from the inside.

But our concentration has been on bloggers. Obviously, they reach people who read. And bloggers are interested because so much blog technology is used and because they are realizing that they are a path around mainstream media (MSM in blogger-speak) for more than just news.

How has the Internet changed the publishing industry? What do you predict for the future?

So far, Amazon has been the biggest change to hit mainstream book publishing. Upstarts like 800ceoread have also used the web extremely well for book publicizing and selling. Online bookstores have an infinite shelf so books don't have to be bestsellers in order to be available for sale. Amazon will list a book by anybody for sale, even prepublication.

But this is just the beginning. Just as musicians have, authors can reach their audience without the help of a mainstream publisher—even with hardcopy if they use print-on-demand capability. Mainstream publishers weren't promoting new authors—with the exception of celebrities—anyway. Now an author can get content to readers with almost no distribution expense. Readers can find authors through blogs that talk about them in addition to or instead of traditional reviews.

The mainstream publishers and reviewers—as slow and stodgy as they are—have been the gatekeepers for readers. Now readers can choose authors on their own, preview content or read it entirely online, chat online with authors whom they may never meet in person. All good stuff from an author's point of view and readers get more choice. Just like the telephone and music industries are finding, publishers will have to adapt to using and facilitating these technologies.

Author Profile: Lee Foster

www.fostertravel.com

Lee Foster is the acknowledged pioneer in travel online-web publishing. He was the first travel writer ever to earn a dollar in the new online scene, starting back in 1983 with CompuServe. His popular Foster Travel Publishing website (**www.fostertravel.com**) presents for consumers and for content buyers more than 200 worldwide destinations. Lee is a veteran travel writer-photographer whose work has won seven Lowell Thomas Awards. As a travel photographer, he has images in more than 225 Lonely Planet books. His most recent Lowell Thomas Award was for a travel guidebook, *Northern California History Weekends* (Globe Pequot). Lee lives in Berkeley, California.

How important is your website in marketing your books?

My website for Foster Travel Publishing is at **www.fostertravel.com**. I present on it travel writing/photography on 200 worldwide destinations. I have two audiences: consumers looking for travel information/insight and content buyers in print or on the web looking for writing or photo travel content (magazines, newspapers, book companies, websites, and so forth).

Note that there is an Order Now button going directly to my secure order form for people who want to buy an autographed copy of any of my seven books. This is especially profitable as a sales vehicle for my independently-published latest book. I process credit card orders through ProPay and receive money through my PayPal account (lee@fostertravel.com) as well as receive mailed checks.

Now consider a typical content page on my website, such as my write-up on Yosemite at **www.fostertravel.com/CAYOSE.html**. Whenever consumers look at my travel content, I have an opportunity to sell them my books. I have Google ads around my content for revenue, but, on the right side of the page, I also have a cover photo and an ad for two of my books, and show how people can go directly to a secure order form or learn more at the press release. This results in incremental sales of the books. According to Metrics Market (**www.metricsmarket.com**), I have about 117,900 monthly visitor sessions with people looking at my content. That means I have 117,900 opportunities a month to sell my book to a consumer, possibly directly, which is quite profitable.

How do you use online press releases to connect with your audience?

As a start, I use my website to present a robust press release about my book. The press release is for consumers as well as the media. See it at **www.fostertravel.com/travels.html**. The press release alerts you to more details. There is a three-chapter sample PDF of my latest book to tease buyers who might want to test drive the book before purchasing. The book can also be purchased as a downloadable PDF, beyond a printed book, or as a PDF on a CD. All these options are possible because of my website and my interaction with buyers through it, using the press release as the vehicle.

The press release also has a 300 dpi photo of the author and the cover permanently available to any media reviewers. This makes it easy for reviewers. Of course, the press release and other places where my book is mentioned on my website have a direct tie in to Amazon.com. I have the usual Associate relationship with Amazon and receive a small incremental fee back from them for sales that come in through my website. I also have the direct Advantage relationship with Amazon for the book I independently publish. These Amazon relationships are profitable and orderly, since they pay with precision on a certain day.

Note in the press release and throughout my website an integrated approach to what I am selling. I am selling travel writing/photo content to consumers and to content buyers. This press release on my book alerts the viewer that I have 200 worldwide write-ups available. When a consumer looks at them and clicks on a Google ad, I get revenue. A consumer may not be interested in my books, but may be interested in my articles. A viewer of this press release may not be interested in my latest book, but may be interested in my earlier books. It is clearly noted that any bookstore can get the books through Baker & Taylor. A content buyer may not be interested in my books, but may want to lease photos for a magazine, and so forth. The message is clear: Lee Foster presents and sells travel writing/photo content in various ways.

How important is an email signature to your online marketing campaign?

Every time an email goes out from me to anyone, my signature alerts people to my new book and the press release on my website. It is important, obviously, to have a well functioning website to take advantage of any interest shown. This is my current signature:

Lee Foster
Foster Travel Publishing
PO Box 5715
Berkeley, CA 94705
510/549-2202
lee@fostertravel.com
www.fostertravel.com

Lee's new literary book is:
Travels in an American Imagination-The Spiritual Geography of Our Time
www.fostertravel.com/travels.html

What impact does the Internet have on independent publishing?

The rise of the Internet and the evolution of book marketing make this a particularly auspicious time to consider independent publishing of books ("independent" is a better word than "self" to describe this strategy). I have three main motivations for independent publishing—greater profit, total control over design and marketing of the book, and assured availability of the book as long as the sun doth shine. All are related to my website and the new era of Internet marketing of books.

What new online book promotion tools are you using?

One new and quirky aspect of the Internet is that you can keep informed on some places that may be publicizing your book through Google Alerts. I signed up for Google Alerts. When I pop up in the news, they tell me about it, for free. When David Armstrong of the *San Francisco Chronicle* did a review on my book, I knew about it before it came out in print. It was on their sfgate.com website. Google Alerts told me about it, for free.

Beware, however, that there are many people with your name, even a less usual name, such as Lee Foster. If you have a common name, you will find that many unsolicited reports of your death, your criminal acts, and your athletic triumphs will be presented to you.

Author Profile: Diana L. Guerrero

www.dianalguerrero.com (media and event-oriented site)
www.arkanimals.com (ezine)
www.whatanimalscanteachusaboutspirituality.com
www.blessingoftheanimals.com

Animal expert and author Diana L. Guerrero is an innovative pioneer whose first word was "fish." Her works and quotes have appeared in zoological journals, pet and veterinary industry publications, and various magazines throughout the world. Guerrero currently resides in the mountains of southern California and is represented by the New York Literary Agency, Bykofsky & Associates. Her books include *What Animals Can Teach Us about Spirituality* (Skylight Paths) and *Blessing of the Animals* (Sterling Publishing).

How much time do you spend on online book promotion as compared to traditional book marketing?

Weekly and sometimes daily effort when in the height of promotion. Traditional book marketing on first book for the general public began three months in advance and continued for a full year.

How important are your website, ezine, and blog in developing an audience for your books?

Critical. During traditional events, I built my readership list by sign-ups. However, I continue to draw potential book buyers and maintain a relationship with my existing fans via the web and monthly electronic newsletter. In addition, my sites attract continuous media inquiries.

What online promotion techniques do you find most effective for attracting media attention? What has been your experience with distributing online press releases and creating an online media kit?

Here's what I do:

- Provide a media site to showcase my credentials, appearances, and coverage
- Provide an educational site to offer information of interest to readership and attract a larger audience
- Provide book-specific sites for event planners and meeting coordinators along with booksellers and community relation managers

I provide commentary on breaking news related to my areas of expertise and when appropriate tie them into my book. I have created perennial topics to assist the media with stories and have an online media kit available for them. In addition, I have an electronic media kit that can be emailed to them with links to everything they need and in a format that is friendly and accessible. I list some segment ideas and encourage them to forward the information to their colleagues.

How do you use website audio and video to promote your books to readers and the media? How have you incorporated podcasting into your online promotion campaign?

I provide both audio and video on my media site. This allows decisions as to whether or not I fit what the producer or interviewer is looking for. I provide audio commentary on breaking news in the form of 60-second PSAs (Public Service Announcements) and podcast these separately from the site. I also use the blog to include tidbits about interesting news bits and link it to the podcast when appropriate.

How effective are teleseminars as a book promotion tool?

I have not used teleseminars as a book promotion tool; rather as a public service and tool to get information to people I might not reach otherwise. The area is still new and growing. I'd suggest contacting Annie Jennings PR (**www.anniejenningspr.com**) regarding their teleseminar success as they have a very large audience and have been of great assistance to myself and many other authors and experts.

Author Profile: Shirley Jump

www.shirleyjump.com

Shirley Jump can't sing, dance, or clap along to "Kumbaya" so she opted for the only career that doesn't require natural rhythm—writing. She sold her first book to Silhouette in 2001 and now writes books about love, family, and food—the three most important things in her life (order reversible, depending on the day)—using that English degree everyone said would be useless. Though she's thrilled to see her books in stores around the world, Shirley mostly writes because it gives her an excuse to avoid cleaning the toilets and helps feed her shoe habit. Some of her recent books include *The Bachelor Preferred Pastry* (Zebra Books) and *The Dating Game* (Silhouette).

How much time do you spend on online book promotion as compared to traditional book marketing?

It depends on the book. For my Silhouette books, there's really no need to do traditional book marketing because Harlequin does quite a bit. Sales of category novels are pretty much dependable and fixed. With those books, I do solely online promotion because it's not a big outlay of cost and it seems to increase sales (going by the increase in my sell-through numbers with recent releases). However, with my single title novels, I do a hefty amount of both, with web marketing being about even with traditional.

How important are online excerpts for attracting new readers?

I think they are unbelievably vital. One of my books was chosen for ChapterADay.com, where they run five excerpts in one week. I had a ton of mail from new readers who said they were dying to read the book because of that excerpt. Sales were good on that book, too, and even better on the next one, so I know there had to be some carryover readers (the publisher had put a teaser in the back of the book for the next one). I have an excerpt up on my site a couple of weeks before the book goes on sale, and then archive all excerpts. Having the old excerpts there has been a big help in exposing people to my backlist; several people have emailed me to say they went out and got the book because of that.

What role do online contests play in generating interest in your books?

I think they get people to visit my site, but I don't think they make an appreciable dent in sales. I used to give away "things" and then realized giving away books was a double win-win (no pun intended). I do a monthly contest through Writerspace, and the majority of the winners are already fans. However, there are people who win the books, get them autographed—and then sell them on eBay. I think the contest just helps you gain exposure, although I have had the occasional loyal fan grow out of winning a copy of my book.

How do you use your website and blog to convey a sense of personality and connect with your audience?

I started with my photos. I went to a professional photographer and had photos taken that looked relaxed and friendly, then built everything else around that. I also had a major redesign of my site done this past summer. I told the web designer that I wanted something that reflected the spirit of that photo, and I think he accomplished it.

My blog is very much about my daily life (but not so much that I end up giving out so much information some crazy can track me down) from my braces ordeal to the death of my mother. I try to make it sound just like me, and to cover the same things I'd talk about in person if we were having a cup of coffee. That's pretty much my whole approach—what would I say, do, look like, if I went out for coffee with a reader.

What online book promotion tool, that you aren't currently using, are you most interested in trying and why?

I don't do a lot of paid web advertising nor do I post a lot on bulletin boards where readers congregate, so I think those are two things I'd increase if I had the time. The biggest problem with all of this is that I am a one-woman shop. I not only write the books, I market the books and do all the bookkeeping for the business and all the minutiae involved in running a small business. It keeps me so busy, that some things inevitably have to fall by the wayside. Now if that cloning project works out… <G> Just kidding.

Author Profile: Tee Morris

www.teemorris.com/blog

Tee Morris entered 2005 with an idea of podcasting *MOREVI* in order to promote its sequel, *Legacy of Morevi*—and went on to become the first book podcast in its entirety. That experience led to the founding of Podiobooks.com and the collaboration with Evo Terra on *Podcasting for Dummies*, the user-friendly, how-to guide to podcasting from Wiley Press. Along with the premiere of that title and *Legacy of MOREVI: Book One of the Arathellean Wars*, Tee also appeared in BenBella Books' *Farscape Forever: Sex, Drugs, and Killer Muppets* and launched *The Survival Guide to Writing Fantasy* podcast. He is also planning a podcast of his novel, *Billibub Baddings and the Case of the Singing Sword.*

How much time do you spend on online book promotion as compared to traditional book marketing?

When I first started promoting myself as an author in 2002, I was aggressive in attacking bookstores and conventions. My goal was to get my name out there. Online, I also worked to established an "Internet presence" with a website that served as an online book proposal, participation with online writing groups, and approaching online book reviewers and book interest websites for reviews, interviews, and advertising options. I would say it was an even split between promotion online and in the real world.

Advertising options, since Dragon Moon Press is a small, independent publisher, fell back to me. I explored conventional print advertising options and online link exchanges and banner ads. It was challenging for me to try and accurately track how many sales were made when I was following this avenue, and I found myself questioning it since I continued to invest in it but saw very little in tangible returns and accurate tracking.

In 2005, I was still touring conventions and bookstores but when I turned to podcasting (and also became a dad in the summer of 2004) I was relying more and more on the Internet to market my work. I still average a SF/F convention a month, but my bookstore visits have been scaled back considerably.

Not that I regret the change. Podcasting, I have found, has already paid for itself in sales, coverage, and experience.

What do you think about podcasting as a viable promotion tool for authors?

Podcasting has the potential and promise to be a new sounding board (pardon the pun) for up-and-coming authors, and a great way for established authors to breathe new life into past favorite works. A huge plus of podcasting is instant global distribution. When you put a chapter into your RSS feed, your work is available to readers around the world. I know since podcasting *MOREVI*, my international sales—which were limited, to say the least—increased. In fact, *MOREVI* is about to turn four years old as a novel, and it is selling just as well now (if not better) than it did when it was released. This is all due to the podcast.

Another terrific bonus of podcasting novels (or creating "podiobooks" as we call them at Podiobooks.com) is that it is easy to do and a lot of fun. There is a strong demand for literary audio content, and this demand comes at a time when only select titles are being tapped for audio production. With podiobooks, authors are in control and are personally giving a voice to their work. It's a lot of fun, especially when the feedback rolls in from chapter to chapter. Good or bad, your listeners are given a chance to participate in the creation of this audio production. The more you improve in your delivery and production values, the more your listeners appreciate it.

Podcasting has been a win-win-win situation for me, and for a fraction of the amount it cost me to buy a year's worth of print advertising, I have earned many print sales and thousands of listeners around the country and the world. It never ceases to amaze (and humble) me.

How has podcasting helped you to connect further with your audience?

In The Survival Guide, my listeners hear how I take on the responsibility of marketing and promoting my works from Dragon Moon, Ben Bella, and Wiley Publishing. I also give listeners a sneak peek at how I market and promote myself, something many authors have been forced to do over the past decades. (And some are better at it than others.) Along with my own stories from the road, I interview other authors from large and small presses, established and new, and of various genres who face the challenges of self-promotion. With the spirit of fun I promote on the show, the audience gets to know the personality behind the imagination, and from here a fan base begins to grow. This kind of rapport is real magic, and an unexpected bonus with podcasting, and it gives your readers a chance to see that writing is more than just sitting in an office, hammering out ideas on a computer, and planning book signings. That inside look is one that is appreciated.

How important are online reviews and excerpts for attracting readers?

Online reviews carry weight, although there is an overwhelming opinion that they do not. To dismiss them is short-sighted, but the argument makes sense. In some cases, especially when the website has no editorial staff, online book reviews are in need of proofreaders. What I hope from any review is a sincerity behind the opinion, whether it is overwhelming positive or deeply critical. Particularly on Amazon.com, reviews help sell books. These aren't people who are paid to review books, but comments from readers who all feel passionately enough about a title to express an opinion.

With excerpts from my books, I always provide the opening of the first chapter. It's a pretty safe bet if I can't grab them in the opening, the reader will have no interest to progress any further. It's always a plus when you can back up a good review with a selection from the book that's getting said review. Websites like Fantasy Novel Review and The Eternal Night are terrific resources to not only get an honest review but also give a preview of your work.

In what ways do you use your website, ezine, and blog to develop an audience for your books?

My website and podcast's blog provide the latest information on what my latest releases are, where you can find them (online, in bookstores, and so forth), and a schedule of appearances at conventions and bookstores. I don't pretend to be a blogging veteran or close to being a blog expert (and truth be told, I was *avoiding* setting up a web log mainly because I didn't want another online commitment…then again, that was before podcasting…), but what I've experienced with *The Survival Guide to Writing Fantasy*'s companion blog is a quick and easy way to post upcoming signings, breaking news, and any random thoughts that hit me in a moment. This is the both a pro and con of blogging. I need to be cautious how much I dedicate to it as I don't want to come in short with my daily development of works-in-progress. (That's what I mean by blogging being a distraction.)

Podcasting, on the other hand, is an investment in time I don't mind making because it is a terrific artistic outlet for me outside of writing. Additionally, I tend to talk faster than I type.

The Internet has always been a phenomenal marketing tool for authors. With podcasting, a new tool is being offered. I feel very fortunate to have tapped into this new media and hope other authors and publishers take advantage of it as well.

What online book promotion tool, that you aren't currently using, are you most interested in trying and why?

If I can find the time, I would like to explore blogging a bit more. My podcast's blog has given me a new appreciation for this; and to some extent, I feel very late to the party. My only concern is, as mentioned a moment ago, time. I need to write. A lot. When I'm not writing, I'm podcasting. When I'm not podcasting, I'm organizing podcasts for Podiobooks.com. When I'm not doing that, I'm living life…something all authors can't forget to do.

Thanks to podcasting, though, my curiosity is piqued, so I've got to see if I can find the time to really invest into it.

Google's AdWords also have me curious. Are they worth the investment? Do people really take advantage of them? What's the true amount of traffic? My partner in *Podcasting for Dummies*, Evo Terra, knows a bit about them, I believe…

Author Profile: Angie Pedersen

www.scrapyourstories.com
angiepedersen.typepad.com

Angie Pedersen is a freelance writer for the scrapbooking industry, with articles featured in both trade and consumer magazines. She is the author of three bestselling books about scrapbook journaling including *The Book of Me: A Guide to Scrapbooking about Yourself*, *Growing Up Me: A Guide to Scrapbooking Childhood Stories*, and her latest, *The Book of Us: A Guide to Scrapbooking about Relationships*. Angie also provides marketing consulting and writing services to small businesses, helping them get noticed by the media and their target market.

How much time do you spend on online book promotion as compared to traditional book marketing?

Almost all of my book promotion has been online; I have done very little offline. Neither my publisher nor I have done any print advertising, nor did I go on any book tours. The day-to-day promotion is done online.

How important are your website, ezine, and blog in developing an audience for your books?

My "online presence" is crucial to developing, and more importantly, maintaining my audience. In the scrapbooking community, much of the word-of-mouth buzz is generated and moved online. People request and offer impromptu reviews on message boards, and share links to authors' websites and blogs for more information. My website is my representative 24/7, providing detailed information about my books and current projects. My newsletter and blogs help me keep in touch with my readers, in a more casual environment, informing them of current projects, seeking feedback, and providing information related to my books' topics. I also have an archive of over 100 articles on my website that offers ideas for creative activities related to my books, providing added value for my readers. If I didn't have a website, newsletter, and/or blog, I would miss out on that contact with my readers, as well as the opportunity to offer the components necessary to online viral marketing.

What online promotion techniques do you find most effective for attracting media attention? What has been your experience with distributing online press releases and creating an online media kit on your website?

Honestly, I don't have concrete proof of my results of having an online press room. My press room provides my bio and picture, links to online book reviews and interviews I've done, and a listing of magazine articles I've written. But I can't point to those resources and definitively say they've resulted in media attention. I know the media have browsed my press resources, looking for background information on me, but I can't say that information has led to an interview or write-up.

That lack of feedback doesn't change my belief that an online press room is very important, however. Distributing press releases online, and archiving them on your website dramatically increases your chances of being noticed by the media. If a reporter is researching an article in your niche, one of her first steps will be to "Google" that industry. If you have your press releases online, that reporter will get a sense of who you are and how you can help her write her article, because you have helped other reporters with their articles. An online press room allows you to present yourself as an informational resource on a specific subject, increasing your chances of being noticed by the media. Use your press room to tell the media how you can help them complete their assignments.

How did your virtual book tour help further connect with your target audience?

My Virtual Book Tour (VBT) allowed me to connect with people far outside of my geographic area, without the expense of actually traveling to meet them. In the space of two weeks, I was able to "travel" to ten different states, as well as the United Kingdom and New Zealand! Of course, the sites provide content to much more than just ten states, furthering my promotional "reach." A typical bookstore signing draws 10 to 50 people. My visit to each website averaged more than 200, and those numbers continue to increase, because the content is still archived on the sites.

Another benefit of my tour was its almost conversational tone. One of my main goals for the tour was to generally make myself available (and approachable). I know many of my readers struggle with specific topics, and I offered to answer questions in chats during my tour. One chat had over 200 attendees! I answered a lot of reader questions, providing them with insight into who I am, why I wrote my books, and how my books might apply to them. Tour participants told me they enjoyed the opportunity to ask questions and get specific feedback in a casual atmosphere—something they wouldn't have been able to do if I hadn't coordinated my online tour.

What online book promotion tool, that you aren't currently using, are you most interested in trying and why?

I'm interested in trying online classes with video. I've found that book sales are often good following my classes, because I'm able to explain how the material found in the books can apply to real-life situations. Teaching classes online allows information to be available 24/7. I've had experience with teaching text/message-board-based classes online, and they work well. But adding a video component would allow me to more accurately express my enthusiasm for my subjects "in person." Video would also help present any hands-on demonstrations I'd want to do.

Author Profile: Paris Permenter and John Bigley

www.lovetripper.com

Paris Permenter and John Bigley are a husband-wife team of travel writers specializing in romantic travel, honeymoons, and destination weddings. The authors of 29 guidebooks, the couple turned their attentions to Internet publishing in 2000 with the Valentine's Day launch of Lovetripper.com, a website devoted to romantic travel, honeymoons, and destination weddings around the world. Today the site has grown to over 5,000 pages and receives close to a million page views per month.

You host a website, Lovetripper.com, specializing in romantic travel. What impact has the success of this site had on the marketing of your books?

The website and the books go hand in hand; we sell both print and ebooks through the website. Lovetripper.com has helped turn us into more of a brand, rather than the authors of guidebooks on a variety of destinations. We've received many interview requests, including television, radio, online, and print, directly because of the website. Because of the press information on the website, we have done two one-hour shows for the Fine Living television network and we've been interviewed by publications ranging from *USA Today* to *The Christian Science Monitor.*

What's your opinion on ebooks as a supplemental revenue stream for authors of traditional print books? What role does affiliate marketing play in ebook success?

Ebooks are an excellent way to supplement online revenue. We have ebook versions of some of our traditional guidebooks, and we also have some books that have only been published in ebook format. Generally, ebook sales are lower than print sales but, for titles which we self-publish as ebooks, sales don't have to be as great for us to make a nice supplemental income. Costs for ebooks are minimal so most of the purchase price is profit, a far cry from print titles.

We sell our ebooks through ClickBank, a service which handles credit card processing for us; they charge us a per book fee for the credit card transaction, but it is well worth the expense. ClickBank also operates our affiliate program, which allows other websites to sell our ebook titles in exchange for a 40 percent payout. Even with the 40 percent payout to affiliates and the credit card fee, we still make more money per sale with ebooks than with print books.

How important are your ezine, blog, and feed in developing an audience for your books?

The website has been extremely important in developing a Lovetripper brand of books. We publish two e-newsletters, which go out twice monthly; these are important for bringing readers back to the website and for introducing new products.

The increasing use of email filters, however, has made it more and more difficult to get e-newsletters in the hands of the readers; many are filtered out before they reach the subscriber's inbox. Because of that, this past year, we added RSS feeds, which we update daily, sometimes several times a day. These have brought thousands of readers to the website and are very easy to produce and update.

What role does an online media kit play in attracting media attention/interviews?

An online media kit is important for getting media attention; it's important to have a press room link on your site to make it simple for journalists to reach you and to make it evident that you seek publicity. We have an online press room with our contact information, a list of recent media appearances and interviews, sample questions, and so forth.

What online book promotion tool, that you aren't currently using, are you most interested in trying and why?

We are especially interested in podcasting. This year, we would like to add audio podcasting and possibly video podcasting to the site, helping to grow the brand and helping to personalize the site.

Author Profile: Dan Poynter

www.ParaPublishing.com

Dan Poynter is an author of more than 100 books, has been a publisher since 1969, and is a Certified Speaking Professional (CSP). He is an evangelist for books, an ombudsman for authors, an advocate for publishers, and the godfather to thousands of successfully-published books. His seminars have been featured on CNN, his books have been pictured in *The Wall Street Journal,* and his story has been told in *US News & World Report.* The media come to Dan because he is the leading authority on book publishing.

How important are your website and ezine in developing an audience for your books?

Essential. They replace brochures and mailings. Your site is your storefront—open to the world 24 hours a day. Your ezine is a constant reminder that brings people to your site.

See **parapublishing.com/sites/para/resources/newsletter.cfm**.

What's your opinion on ebooks as a supplemental revenue stream for authors of print books?

We publish several of our titles as ebooks and, because I travel constantly, I read a lot of ebooks. Ebooks, audio books, large print books, and so forth allow you to wring more value out of your basic work. Books are going electronic. Some bound books will soon be as dead as the trees they are printed on.

See **parapublishing.com/sites/para/resources/allproducts.cfm**.

What online promotion techniques do you find most effective for attracting media attention? How important is an online media kit on an author's website?

Think digital and think automation. Computerization saves you time and money. Our ezines are essential. Our website document delivery is automated. We do not print media kits; we post our media kit on our site.

See **parapublishing.com/sites/para/resources/pressroom.cfm**.

What do you think about podcasting as a viable promotion tool for authors?

It is all about content. Why should anyone want to listen to your podcast? Why should anyone want to read your ezine? Podcasts are like ezines, they have to be good to attract listeners (or readers).

How has the Internet changed the publishing industry? What do you predict for the future?

The Internet has lowered costs, made it easier for people all over the world looking for specific info to find us, and automated info-dissemination. Publishers are in the information business and the Internet is about disseminating information. Today there are only two types of publishers: those in danger of missing the electronic boat and those who do not even know there is a boat to catch.

Author Profile: Stephanie Roberts

www.FastFengShui.com

Stephanie Roberts is the author of the popular Fast Feng Shui books, *The Pocket Idiot's Guide to Feng Shui*, and the Clutter-Free Forever! Home Coaching Program. Her most recent book is *Fast Feng Shui for Your Home Office*. Stephanie and her husband are the founding partners of Lotus Pond Press. Her first novel is undergoing a lengthy gestation.

What impact does the Internet have on your ability to promote your books and connect with your audience?

Our business is 100 percent structured around the Internet and online marketing; it is how we promote our products and connect with our audience.

My husband and I are business partners: I'm the writer/publisher, and he's the Internet marketer/web designer. My Fast Feng Shui book series is the core product we promote through our FastFengShui website, and we have related websites (FengShuiEbooks.com and ClutterFreeForever.com, among others) that promote our digital products. We have a global audience of more than 12,000 for my biweekly feng shui ezine, which is a key marketing tool. We also have other online businesses, separate from publishing.

The Internet allows us to be profitably self-employed on our own terms, provides me with complete creative control over my books, and enables me to run our publishing business on a part-time basis so I have time to write more books and develop more websites. Without the Internet, we'd have to go out and get day jobs—gaah!

How much time do you spend on online book promotion as compared to traditional book marketing?

We do 100 percent online marketing and no traditional marketing. This doesn't mean we see no value in traditional marketing. I'm sure I could sell more softcover books if we did more traditional marketing. But softcovers aren't where the profit margin is for us, and traditional marketing doesn't interest, motivate, or inspire us. After 20 years in New York City, I'm deeply into staying relaxed about everything now that I live in Hawaii—which means that getting up at 3 AM local time to do a morning radio show on the mainland isn't something I'm eager to do.

For the first year after I founded Lotus Pond Press, I followed all the typical small press/author book marketing advice and tried to do things the "traditional" way, but I don't have the temperament for it and I ended up stressed and miserable. So I looked at my husband and said, "The h___ with this, let's focus on the Internet." We haven't done any traditional marketing in about four years now, our business continues to prosper, my stress level is practically invisible it's so low, and I really enjoy what I do every day.

What's your opinion on ebooks as a supplemental revenue stream for print books?

For us it's the other way around. Ebooks and digital products are the core of our publishing business. Softcovers are a supplemental revenue stream. One of our most popular products—my Clutter-Free Forever! Home Coaching Program—is only available as a digital product. (I might change my mind about that some day, but for now it's digital-only.)

I produce softcover editions of the Fast Feng Shui books as a courtesy for customers who prefer that format. It's a nice addition to our income, but secondary at best. We made more money from affiliate commissions and Google AdSense (both are important revenue streams for us) than we did from softcover book sales last year. Since we don't target traditional "brick and mortar" bookstores at all, most of our softcover sales are through the major online booksellers.

Ebooks, in our experience, are definitely a complementary (not competitive) product. Our earlier titles were available in softcover before the ebook editions came out, and we saw softcover sales go up after the ebooks became available. I know some people are concerned that offering an ebook will undercut bookstore sales, but that's really not the case. Ebooks appear to reach a different market segment. Whether that will remain true over time, no one knows yet.

I mostly view the softcover editions as marketing tools that do two important things: they enable us to maintain that critical "usually ships in 24 hours" visibility at Amazon.com, and they support foreign rights sales for our titles (another important supplemental revenue stream!). One of my business goals is to eventually be 100 percent digital. For now, softcovers still have a role to play for us, but it's increasingly a marketing role, not an income role.

How important are your ezine and blog in developing your audience?

Very important. But in order to get subscribers, we need website traffic. So search engine optimization, online article circulation (which we do a lot of, and would do more of if I produced more articles more quickly), and PPC are critical to building traffic. I also strongly promote our websites in our print and digital products, so someone who purchases my clutter program will learn about the feng shui site, and feng shui readers will learn about the clutter program, and so on. The more websites we develop the more cross-promotion we do. We also participate in joint ventures with other online publishers/authors, providing short ebook products for other people's bonus packages. We get quite a few ezine subscribers through those promotions, and of course they help to drive sales as well.

What online book promotion tool, that you aren't currently using, are you most interested in trying and why?

I'm interested in exploring a fuller use of multimedia in some way. We have excellent results with audio and video on some of our other (non-publishing) websites, so I'm sure it could be a valuable addition to our book marketing. I don't know if or when we'll get to it, though. There are a lot of things higher on my priority list right now: finishing *Fast Feng Shui for Your Home Office*, turning my half-baked novel into something that resembles a final draft, and creating new websites for the half-dozen URLs we've registered for future business ideas, but haven't done anything with yet.

Glossary

A

Affiliate marketing

An online marketing program in which revenue is shared between a merchant and a company or individual, known as an affiliate, that promotes the merchant's product. Affiliates receive commission payments for sales derived from traffic they direct to the merchant's website.

Aggregator

See *feed reader* or *podcatcher*.

ALT tag

An HTML tag that displays alternative text when an image doesn't display on your website. ALT tags improve site navigation, assist visitors with slow Internet connections, and enhance site accessibility for disabled visitors

Anchor text

The link text of a hyperlink, which a user clicks. Used by search engines to determine relevancy and ranking.

Article marketing

The process of publishing short articles related to your book's subject matter and making these articles available for free reprint to other websites and ezines.

Audioblog

A blog that consists primarily of audio posts.

Autoresponder

A program that is set up to automatically respond to email sent to a specific email address.

B

Banner ad

A graphical web advertisement, available in a variety of sizes. Often is animated.

Blog

Short for weblog, an online journal with content consisting of dated journal entries.

Blog feed

A document that contains summaries of your blog posts, to which people can subscribe and read with a feed reader. Also referred to as an RSS feed.

Blogger

An individual who blogs.

Blogosphere

The totality of all blogs on the Internet.

Blogroll

A list of blogs you read and recommend, often displayed in a blog sidebar.

Blogstorm

Extensive blog coverage on a particular hot topic.

Blook

A book that's derived from or delivered via a blog.

Book Trailer

A short web video used as a promotional tool for books, similar to a movie trailer. Often combines still images, audio, video, and animation.

Browser

Software used to view a website. Internet Explorer, Firefox, and Netscape are common browsers.

C

Call to action

Web copy that encourages a website visitor or email recipient to take a desired action, such as purchase a product or sign up for an ezine.

Chicklet

A small button used to add feed subscription functionality to a blog or website. A chicklet can be a standard feed button or a button for a specific feed reader such as Bloglines, NewsGator, or My Yahoo!

CPC (Cost-per-Click)

The agreed price an online advertiser pays when a user clicks through to a target website.

Crawler

See *spider*.

D

Description tag

An HTML meta tag that describes a specific web page. Some search engines use the text in your description tag in search results; others use text from the body of your web page or create their own description.

Digital download

A downloadable product that you can sell from a website, such as an ebook, software, or audio file.

Domain name

The unique name displayed in a URL to identify a website, such as **www.websavvywriter.com**.

DRM (Digital Rights Management)
A system protecting the copyright of digital media such as ebooks or audio. A DRM system can restrict the access, duplication, distribution, and printing of digital media.

E

Ebook
An electronic book, most commonly formatted as a PDF.

Ecommerce
The sale and purchase of goods and services on the Internet.

Email marketing
The business of promoting products and services via email.

Ezine
An online newsletter, primarily distributed via email. Derived from the term electronic magazine.

F

Feed
A document that contains summaries of your blog posts, podcast, or other web content, to which people can subscribe and read with a feed reader. Also called an RSS feed.

Feed reader
A website or software program that enables you to read and subscribe to feeds. Also called an aggregator.

Flash
Adobe software program designed to create web animations that require limited bandwidth and are browser independent.

G

GIF (Graphics Interchange Format)
Digital image file format that compresses images with few colors such as logos or line drawings.

H

HTML (HyperText Markup Language)
The language used to create pages displayed on the World Wide Web and viewed via a web browser such as Internet Explorer or Firefox.

Home page
The main page of a website. Also referred to as an index page.

I

Internet
A network of millions of computers around the world.

iPod
A portable digital media player developed by Apple.

ISP (Internet service provider)

An organization that provides Internet access, either via dial-up or high speed. Popular ISPs include AOL and EarthLink.

J

JPEG (Joint Photographic Experts Group)

Digital image file format that compresses color and grayscale images; suited to compressing photographs.

K

Keyword

A word used to search for information in a search engine.

Keyword density

The measurement of the ratio of a selected keyword to the rest of the words on a website page. For example, if you use a target word five times in a 120-word web page, the keyword density for that target word is 4 percent.

Keywords tag

An HTML meta tag that lists the keywords for a specific page. Many search engines now ignore the keywords meta tag.

L

Landing page

The page a user arrives at after clicking link text on a website or in an email. Most often used for online text ads.

Link popularity

A measurement of the number of web pages that link to another website. Used by search engines to determine ranking.

M

Message board

An online community in which users post messages on a common topic of interest. Also referred to as a discussion board, forum, bulletin board, or discussion group.

Meta tag

An HTML tag placed in the head section of a web page's HTML code that specifies information about that page. The description tag and keywords tag are common meta tags.

Moblog

A mobile blog, in which blog posts come from a mobile phone or PDA.

MP3 (MPEG Audio Layer 3)

A popular digital audio compression format. Also refers to audio files compressed in this format.

MP3 player
A portable digital audio player that stores and plays digital music and audio files compressed in the MP3 format.

O

Online portfolio
A web-based showcase for writing and other creative samples.

Online press release
A press release distributed on the web that targets both the media and the general public reading online news sites.

Opt-in email
Email that the recipient requests, such as by subscribing to an ezine.

P

Page Rank
Google's ranking of a website's popularity and quality on a scale of 0 to 10.

Permalink
A static address for a blog posting.

Photoblog
A blog that consists primarily of photos.

Ping
To notify web directories and search engines that a blog has new content.

Podcast
An on-demand Internet broadcast, formatted as an MP3 and usually delivered via a feed. Derived from the words iPod and broadcast, but plays on personal computers and other MP3 players in addition to iPods.

Podcatcher
A computer program that enables you to subscribe to, download, and transfer a podcast to a digital audio player. Podcatchers are also called podcast readers, podcast receivers, and aggregators.

Podiobook
A serialized audio book delivered as a podcast.

Podvertising
Advertising on a podcast. Also called advercasting.

PPC (Pay-per-Click)
Online advertising payment method based on paying a specified amount for each click through to a designated web page.

PDF (Portable Document Format)
A popular electronic document format developed by Adobe Systems.

Privacy policy
A published document stating the policy of a website regarding its use of personal information.

R

Reciprocal links
Links between two websites, based on an agreement between their webmasters.

Resource box
An author bio that appears at the end of an article used for article marketing.

Robots tag
A meta tag used to tag pages that you do *not* want search engines to spider.

RSS (Really Simple Syndication)
A syndication format that enables you to provide regular updates to blogs, podcasts, and website content through a feed.

RSS feed
See *feed*.

S

Screencast
An online demo or tutorial presented as a video or Flash movie.

Search engine optimization (SEO)
Techniques used to achieve a top ranking in search engine results for specific keywords.

Search engine
Online software program that searches for web pages matching specific keywords a user enters. Google and Yahoo! are two of the most popular search engines.

Shopping cart
Website software that enables site visitors to view, select, and purchase items available in an online store.

Signature file
A text block at the end of an email message or message board posting that provides additional information about the author.

Site builder
An online tool that enables the quick and easy creation of a website without the need to purchase web-authoring software.

Sitemap
A website page that includes links to all the pages on your site, categorized by topic.

Spam
Unwanted commercial email.

Spider
An automated program that travels the web, indexing results for a search engine. Also called a crawler or robot.

Streaming media
Web-based audio or video that plays and transfers to the web at the same time, providing immediate access without waiting for a file to download.

T

Teleseminar
A live telephone seminar. Often recorded and repackaged as an MP3.

Template
A document or file with a set format that can be reused and customized. Templates are available for many popular software programs to create websites, presentations, and newsletters.

Title tag
Text that appears in a browser's title bar when viewing a web page.

Trackback
A feature enabling you to notify another blog that you linked to one of its posts, in return receiving a link back to your blog.

U

URL (Uniform Resource Locator)
An address on the web, such as **www.websavvywriter.com** or **www.google.com**.

V

Video podcast
A podcast that delivers video instead of audio content. Also referred to as a vidcast, vodcast, videocast, or vcast.

Viral marketing
Word-of-mouth marketing via the Internet or email.

Virtual book tour
An online book promotion tour, with tour "stops" at websites and blogs instead of traditional bookstores.

Vlog
A video blog, in which blog posts are primarily in a video format.

W

Web host

A company that provides server space and related services for websites. Not the same as an ISP, although some ISPs do offer web hosting services.

Website traffic

The number of visitors a website receives.

Website

A unique location on the World Wide Web, containing a home page plus additional pages. Most frequently designated by a specific domain name, such as **www.websavvywriter.com**.

World Wide Web

A linked network of web servers supporting web pages formatted in HTML, which are accessible via a browser. Popularly referred to as "the web." The World Wide Web is part of the Internet, not a synonym for the Internet.

Index

Lightning Source UK Ltd.
Milton Keynes UK
13 October 2009

144870UK00001B/26/P